Mastering Ceph

Redefine your storage system

Nick Fisk

BIRMINGHAM - MUMBAI

Mastering Ceph

First published: May 2017

Production reference: 1260517

Published by Packt Publishing Ltd.
Livery Place
35 Livery Street
Birmingham
B3 2PB, UK.

ISBN 978-1-78588-878-6

www.packtpub.com

Credits

Author
Nick Fisk

Reviewer
Vladimir Franciz S. Blando

Commissioning Editor
Pratik Shah

Acquisition Editor
Meeta Rajani

Content Development Editor
Juliana Nair

Technical Editor
Gaurav Suri

Copy Editor
Dipti Mankame

Project Coordinator
Judie Jose

Proofreader
Safis Editing

Indexer
Rekha Nair

Graphics
Kirk D'Penha

Production Coordinator
Aparna Bhagat

About the Author

Nick Fisk is an IT specialist with a strong history in enterprise storage. Having worked in a variety of roles throughout his career, he has encountered a wide variety of technologies. In 2012, Nick was given the opportunity to focus more toward open source technologies, and this is when his first exposure to Ceph happened. Having seen the potential of Ceph as a storage platform and the benefits of moving away from the traditional closed-stack storage platforms, Nick pursued Ceph with a keen interest.

Throughout the following years, his experience with Ceph increased with the deployment of several clusters and enabled him to spend time in the Ceph community, helping others and improving certain areas of Ceph.

I would firstly like to thank my wife for allowing me to dedicate time to writing this book and to Juliana Nair for supporting me through the writing process.
I would also like to especially thank Tarquin Dunn for the continual support and encouragement he has given me from the initial adoption of Ceph as a storage platform. His support has enabled me to both learn and contribute to this amazing open source project.

About the Reviewer

Vladimir Franciz S. Blando is a seasoned IT professional with 18 years' experience of Linux systems administration, including architecture, design, installation, configuration, and maintenance, working on both bare-metal and virtualized environments. He is well versed in Amazon Web Services, OpenStack cloud, Ceph storage, and other cloud technologies.

I would like to thank Morphlabs for giving me the opportunity to work on various cloud technologies, especially OpenStack and Ceph, and for supporting me all throughout.

www.PacktPub.com

For support files and downloads related to your book, please visit www.PacktPub.com.

Did you know that Packt offers eBook versions of every book published, with PDF and ePub files available? You can upgrade to the eBook version at www.PacktPub.com and as a print book customer, you are entitled to a discount on the eBook copy. Get in touch with us at service@packtpub.com for more details.

At www.PacktPub.com, you can also read a collection of free technical articles, sign up for a range of free newsletters and receive exclusive discounts and offers on Packt books and eBooks.

https://www.packtpub.com/mapt

Get the most in-demand software skills with Mapt. Mapt gives you full access to all Packt books and video courses, as well as industry-leading tools to help you plan your personal development and advance your career.

Why subscribe?

- Fully searchable across every book published by Packt
- Copy and paste, print, and bookmark content
- On demand and accessible via a web browser

Customer Feedback

Thanks for purchasing this Packt book. At Packt, quality is at the heart of our editorial process. To help us improve, please leave us an honest review on this book's Amazon page at `https://www.amazon.com/dp/1785888781`.

If you'd like to join our team of regular reviewers, you can e-mail us at `customerreviews@packtpub.com`. We award our regular reviewers with free eBooks and videos in exchange for their valuable feedback. Help us be relentless in improving our products!

Table of Contents

Preface

Ceph, a unified, highly resilient, distributed storage system that provides block, object, and file access, has enjoyed a surge in popularity over the last few years. Due to being open source, Ceph has enjoyed rapid adoption both from developers and end users alike, with several well-known corporations being involved in the project. With every new release, the scale of its performance and feature set continues to grow, further enhancing Ceph's status.

With the current ever-increasing data storage requirements and challenges faced by legacy RAID-based systems, Ceph is well placed to offer an answer to these problems. As the world moves forward adopting new cloud technologies and object-based storage, Ceph is ready and waiting to be the driving force as part of the new era of storage technologies.

In this book, we will cover a wide variety of topics, from installing and managing a Ceph cluster to how to recover from disasters, should you ever find yourself in that situation. For those that have interest in getting their applications to talk directly to Ceph, this book will also show you how to develop applications that make use of Ceph's libraries and even how to perform distributed computing by inserting your own code into Ceph. By the end of this book, you will be well on your way to mastering Ceph.

What this book covers

Chapter 1, *Planning for Ceph*, covers the basics of how Ceph works, its basic architecture, and what some good use cases are. It also discusses the steps that one should take to plan before implementing Ceph, including design goals, proof of concept, and infrastructure design.

Chapter 2, *Deploying Ceph*, is a no-nonsense step-by-step instructional chapter on how to set up a Ceph cluster. This chapter covers the ceph-deploy tool for testing and goes onto covering Ansible. A section on change management is also included, and it explains how this is essential for the stability of large Ceph clusters. This chapter also serves the purpose of providing you with a common platform you can use for examples later in the book.

Chapter 3, *BlueStore*, explains that Ceph has to be able to provide atomic operations around data and metadata and how filestore was built to provide these guarantees on top of standard filesystems. We will also cover the problems around this approach. The chapter then introduces BlueStore and explains how it works and the problems that it solves. This will include the components and how they interact with different types of storage devices. We will also have an overview of key-value stores, including RocksDB, which is used by BlueStore. Some of the BlueStore settings and how they interact with different hardware configurations will be discussed.

Chapter 4, *Erasure Coding for Better Storage Efficiency*, covers how erasure coding works and how it's implemented in Ceph, including explanations of RADOS pool parameters and erasure coding profiles. A reference to the changes in the Kraken release will highlight the possibility of append-overwrites to erasure pools, which will allow RBDs to directly function on erasure-coded pools. Performance considerations will also be explained. This will include references to BlueStore, as it is required for sufficient performance. Finally, we have step-by-step instructions on actually setting up erasure coding on a pool, which can be used as a mechanical reference for sysadmins.

Chapter 5, *Developing with Librados*, explains how Librados is used to build applications that can interact directly with a Ceph cluster. It then moves onto several different examples of using Librados in different languages to give you an idea of how it can be used, including atomic transactions.

Chapter 6, *Distributed Computation with Ceph RADOS Classes*, discusses the benefits of moving processing directly into the OSD to effectively perform distributed computing. It then covers how to get started with RADOS classes by building simple ones with Lua. It then covers how to build your own C++ RADOS class into the Ceph source tree and conduct benchmarks against performing processing on the client versus the OSD.

Chapter 7, *Monitoring Ceph*, starts with a description of why monitoring is important and discusses the difference between alerting and monitoring. The chapter will then cover how to obtain performance counters from all the Ceph components and explain what some of the key counters mean and how to convert them into usable values.

Chapter 8, *Tiering with Ceph*, explains how RADOS tiering works in Ceph, where it should be used, and its pitfalls. It takes you step-by-step through configuring tiering on a Ceph cluster and finally covers the tuning options to extract the best performance for tiering. An example using Graphite will demonstrate the value of being able to manipulate captured data to provide more meaningful output in graph form.

Chapter 9, *Tuning Ceph*, starts with a brief overview of how to tune Ceph and the operating system. It also covers basic concepts of avoiding trying to tune something that is not a bottleneck. It will also cover the areas that you may wish to tune and establish how to gauge the success of tuning attempts. Finally, it will show you how to benchmark Ceph and take baseline measurements so that any results achieved are meaningful. We'll discuss different tools and how benchmarks might relate to real-life performance.

Chapter 10, *Troubleshooting*, explains how although Ceph is largely autonomous in taking care of itself and recovering from failure scenarios, in some cases, human intervention is required. We'll look at common errors and failure scenarios and how to bring Ceph back to full health by troubleshooting them.

Chapter 11, *Disaster Recovery*, covers situations when Ceph is in such a state that there is a complete loss of service or data loss has occurred. Less familiar recovery techniques are required to restore access to the cluster and, hopefully, recover data. This chapter arms you with the knowledge to attempt recovery in these scenarios.

What you need for this book

This book assumes medium-level knowledge of Linux operating systems and basic knowledge of storage technologies and networking. Although the book will go through a simple multi-node setup of a Ceph cluster, it is advisable that you have some prior experience of using Ceph. Although the book uses VirtualBox, feel free to use any other lab environment, such as VMware Workstation.

This book requires that you have enough resources to run the whole Ceph lab environment. The minimum hardware or virtual requirements are as follows:

- CPU: 2 cores
- Memory: 8 GB RAM
- Disk space: 40 GB

You will need the following software:

- VirtualBox
- Vagrant

Internet connectivity is required to install the packages that are part of the examples in each chapter.

Who this book is for

To make use of the content of this book, basic prior knowledge of Ceph is expected. If you feel you don't have that knowledge, it is always possible to catch up with the basics by having a quick read of the major components from the official Ceph documentation, `http://docs.ceph.com/docs/master/`. This book is essentially intended for Ceph cluster administrators. If you are already running a Ceph cluster, this book can help you to gain a better understanding.

Conventions

In this book, you will find a number of text styles that distinguish between different kinds of information. Here are some examples of these styles and an explanation of their meaning.

Code words in text, database table names, folder names, filenames, file extensions, pathnames, dummy URLs, user input, and Twitter handles are shown as follows: "Learning about the differences between `ceph-deploy` and orchestration tools."

A block of code is set as follows:

```
nodes = [
  { :hostname => 'ansible', :ip => '192.168.0.40', :box => 'xenial64'
  },
  { :hostname => 'mon1', :ip => '192.168.0.41', :box => 'xenial64' },
  { :hostname => 'mon2', :ip => '192.168.0.42', :box => 'xenial64' },
  { :hostname => 'mon3', :ip => '192.168.0.43', :box => 'xenial64' },
```

Any command-line input or output is written as follows:

```
vagrant plugin install vagrant-hostmanager
```

New terms and **important words** are shown in bold. Words that you see on the screen, for example, in menus or dialog boxes, appear in the text like this: "It has probed OSDs 1 and 2 for the data, which means that it didn't find anything it needed. It wants to try and pol OSD 0, but it can't because the OSD is down, hence the message as **starting or marking this osd lost may let us proceed appeared**."

Warnings or important notes appear in a box like this.

Tips and tricks appear like this.

Reader feedback

Feedback from our readers is always welcome. Let us know what you think about this book-what you liked or disliked. Reader feedback is important for us as it helps us develop titles that you will really get the most out of.

To send us general feedback, simply e-mail feedback@packtpub.com, and mention the book's title in the subject of your message.

If there is a topic that you have expertise in and you are interested in either writing or contributing to a book, see our author guide at www.packtpub.com/authors.

Customer support

Now that you are the proud owner of a Packt book, we have a number of things to help you to get the most from your purchase.

Downloading the example code

You can download the example code files for this book from your account at http://www.packtpub.com. If you purchased this book elsewhere, you can visit http://www.packtpub.com/support and register to have the files e-mailed directly to you.

You can download the code files by following these steps:

1. Log in or register to our website using your e-mail address and password.
2. Hover the mouse pointer on the **SUPPORT** tab at the top.
3. Click on **Code Downloads & Errata**.
4. Enter the name of the book in the **Search** box.

5. Select the book for which you're looking to download the code files.
6. Choose from the drop-down menu where you purchased this book from.
7. Click on **Code Download**.

Once the file is downloaded, please make sure that you unzip or extract the folder using the latest version of:

- WinRAR / 7-Zip for Windows
- Zipeg / iZip / UnRarX for Mac
- 7-Zip / PeaZip for Linux

The code bundle for the book is also hosted on GitHub at `https://github.com/PacktPubl ishing/Mastering-Ceph`. We also have other code bundles from our rich catalog of books and videos available at `https://github.com/PacktPublishing/`. Check them out!

Downloading the color images of this book

We also provide you with a PDF file that has color images of the screenshots/diagrams used in this book. The color images will help you better understand the changes in the output. You can download this file from `https://www.packtpub.com/sites/default/files/down loads/MasteringCeph_ColorImages.pdf`.

Errata

Although we have taken every care to ensure the accuracy of our content, mistakes do happen. If you find a mistake in one of our books-maybe a mistake in the text or the code- we would be grateful if you could report this to us. By doing so, you can save other readers from frustration and help us improve subsequent versions of this book. If you find any errata, please report them by visiting `http://www.packtpub.com/submit-errata`, selecting your book, clicking on the **Errata Submission Form** link, and entering the details of your errata. Once your errata are verified, your submission will be accepted and the errata will be uploaded to our website or added to any list of existing errata under the Errata section of that title.

To view the previously submitted errata, go to `https://www.packtpub.com/books/conten t/support`and enter the name of the book in the search field. The required information will appear under the **Errata** section.

Piracy

Piracy of copyrighted material on the Internet is an ongoing problem across all media. At Packt, we take the protection of our copyright and licenses very seriously. If you come across any illegal copies of our works in any form on the Internet, please provide us with the location address or website name immediately so that we can pursue a remedy.

Please contact us at copyright@packtpub.com with a link to the suspected pirated material.

We appreciate your help in protecting our authors and our ability to bring you valuable content.

Questions

If you have a problem with any aspect of this book, you can contact us at questions@packtpub.com, and we will do our best to address the problem.

1
Planning for Ceph

The first chapter of this book covers all the areas you need to consider when looking to deploy a Ceph cluster from initial planning stages to hardware choices. Topics covered in this chapter are as follows:

- What Ceph is and how it works
- Good use cases for Ceph and important considerations
- Advice and best practices on infrastructure design
- Ideas around planning a Ceph project

What is Ceph?

Ceph is an open source, distributed, scale-out, **software-defined storage (SDS)** system, which can provide block, object, and file storage. Through the use of the **Controlled Replication Under Scalable Hashing (CRUSH)** algorithm, Ceph eliminates the need for centralized metadata and can distribute the load across all the nodes in the cluster. Since CRUSH is an algorithm, data placement is calculated rather than being based on table lookups and can scale to hundreds of petabytes without the risk of bottlenecks and the associated single points of failure. Clients also form direct connections with the server storing the requested data and so their is no centralised bottleneck in the data path.

Ceph provides the three main types of storage, being block via **RADOS Block Devices (RBD)**, file via **Ceph Filesystem (CephFS)**, and object via the **Reliable Autonomous Distributed Object Store (RADOS)** gateway, which provides **Simple Storage Service (S3)** and **Swift** compatible storage.

Ceph is a pure SDS solution and as such means that you are free to run it on commodity hardware as long as it provides the correct guarantees around data consistency. More information on the recommended types of hardware can be found later on in this chapter. This is a major development in the storage industry which has typically suffered from strict vendor lock-in. Although there have been numerous open source projects to provide storage services. Very few of them have been able to offer the scale and high resilience of Ceph, without requiring propriety hardware.

It should be noted that Ceph prefers consistency as per the **CAP theorem** and will try at all costs to make protecting your data the biggest priority over availability in the event of a partition.

How Ceph works?

The core storage layer in Ceph is RADOS, which provides, as the name suggests, an object store on which the higher level storage protocols are built and distributed. The RADOS layer in Ceph comprises a number of OSDs. Each OSD is completely independent and forms peer-to-peer relationships to form a cluster. Each OSD is typically mapped to a single physical disk via a basic **host bus adapter (HBA)** in contrast to the traditional approach of presenting a number of disks via a **Redundant Array of Independent Disks (RAID)** controller to the OS.

The other key component in a Ceph cluster are the monitors; these are responsible for forming cluster quorum via the use of **Paxos**. By forming quorum the monitors can be sure that are in a state where they are allowed to make authoritative decisions for the cluster and avoid split brain scenarios. The monitors are not directly involved in the data path and do not have the same performance requirements as OSDs. They are mainly used to provide a known cluster state including membership, configuration, and statistics via the use of various cluster maps. These cluster maps are used by both Ceph cluster components and clients to describe the cluster topology and enable data to be safely stored in the right location.

Due to the scale that Ceph is intended to be operated at, one can appreciate that tracking the state and placement of every single object in the cluster would become computationally very expensive. Ceph solves this problem using CRUSH to place the objects into groups of objects named **placement groups (PGs)**. This reduces the need to track millions of objects to a much more manageable number in the thousands range.

Librados is a Ceph library that can be used to build applications that interact directly with the RADOS cluster to store and retrieve objects.

For more information on how the internals of Ceph work, it would be strongly recommended to read the official Ceph documentation and also the thesis written by Sage Weil, the creator and primary architect of Ceph.

Ceph use cases

Before jumping into a specific use case, let's cover some key points that should be understood and considered before thinking about deploying a Ceph cluster.

Replacing your storage array with Ceph

Ceph should not be compared with a traditional scale-up storage array. It is fundamentally different, and trying to shoehorn Ceph into that role using existing knowledge, infrastructure, and expectation will lead to disappointment. Ceph is **Software Defined Storage (SDS)** whose internal data movements operate over TCP/IP networking. This introduces several extra layers of technology and complexity compared with a SAS cable at the rear of a traditional storage array.

Performance

Due to Ceph's distributed approach, it can offer unrestrained performance compared with scale-up storage arrays, which typically have to funnel all I/O through a pair of controller heads. Although technology has constantly been providing new faster CPUs and faster network speeds, there is still a limit to the performance you can expect to achieve with just a pair of controllers. With recent advances in flash technology combined with new interfaces such as **Non-volatile Memory Express (NVMe)**, the scale-out nature of Ceph provides a linear increase in CPU and network resource with every added OSD node.

Let us also consider where Ceph is not a good fit for performance, and this is mainly around use cases where extremely low latency is desired. For the very reason that enables Ceph to become a scale-out solution, it also means that low latency performance will suffer. The overhead of software and additional network hops means that latency will tend to be about double that of a traditional storage array and 10 times that of local storage. A thought should be given to selecting the best technology for given performance requirements. That said, a well-designed and tuned Ceph cluster should be able to meet performance requirements in all but the most extreme cases.

Object storage with custom application

Using librados, you can get your in-house application to directly talk to the underlying Ceph RADOS layer. This can greatly simplify the development of your application and gives you direct access to highly performant reliable storage. Some of the more advanced features of librados, which allow you to bundle a number of operations into a single atomic operation, are also very hard to do with existing storage solutions.

Distributed filesystem – web farm

A farm of web servers all need to access the same files so that they can all serve the same content no matter which one the client connects to. Traditionally, a **high-availability (HA)** NFS solution would be used to provide distributed file access but can start to hit several limitations at scale. CephFS can provide a distributed filesystem to store the web content and allow it to be mounted across all the web servers in the farm.

Distributed filesystem – SMB file server replacement

There are several interactions between CephFS and Samba, which have not been refined, meaning that the end solution would not work as well as expected. Samba can successfully be used to present a CephFS filesystem, but the lack of HA and stable snapshots means that it will often be a poor replacement. As of the publication of this book, this is not currently a recommended use case for Ceph.

Infrastructure design

While considering infrastructure design we need to take care of certain components. We will now briefly look at this components.

SSDs

SSDs are great. They have come down enormously in price over the past 10 years, and every evidence suggests that they will continue to do so. They have the ability to offer access times several orders of magnitude lower than rotating disks and consume less power.

One important concept to understand about SSDs is that although their read and write latencies are typically measured in 10's of microseconds, to overwrite an existing data in a flash block, it requires the entire flash block to be erased before the write can happen. A typical flash block size in SSD may be 128 KB, and even a 4 KB write I/O would require the entire block to be read, erased and then the existing data and new I/O to be finally written. The erase operation can take several milliseconds and without clever routines in the SSD firmware, would make writes painfully slow. To get around this limitation, SSDs are equipped with a RAM buffer, so they can acknowledge writes instantly, whereas the firmware internally moves data around flash blocks to optimize the overwrite process and wear leveling. However, the RAM buffer is volatile memory and would normally result in the possibility of data loss and corruption in the event of sudden power loss. To protect against this, SSDs can have power loss protection, which is accomplished by having a large capacitor on board, to store enough power to flush any outstanding writes to flash.

One of the biggest trends in recent years is the different tiers of SSDs that have become available. Broadly speaking, these can be broken down into the following categories.

Consumer

These are the cheapest you can buy and are pitched at the average PC user. They provide a lot of capacity very cheaply and offer fairly decent performance. They will likely offer no power loss protection and will either demonstrate extremely poor performance when asked to do synchronous writes or lie about stored data integrity. They will also likely have very poor write endurance, but still more than enough for standard use.

Prosumer

These are a step up from the consumer models and will typically provide better performance and have higher write endurance although still far off what enterprise SSDs provide.

Before moving on to the enterprise models, it is worth just covering why you should not under any condition use the earlier-mentioned models of SSDs for Ceph:

- Lack of proper power loss protection will either result in extremely poor performance or not ensure proper data consistency
- Firmware is not as heavily tested as enterprise SSDs often revealing data corrupting bugs

- Low write endurance will mean that they will quickly wear out, often ending in sudden failure
- Due to high wear and failure rates, their initial cost benefits rapidly disappear

The use of consumer SSDs with Ceph will result in poor performance and increase the chance of catastrophic data loss.

Enterprise SSDs

The biggest difference between consumer and enterprise SSDs is that an enterprise SSD should provide the guarantee that when it responds to the host system confirming that data has been safely stored, it actually is. That is to say, that if power is suddenly removed from a system all data that the operating system believes was committed to disk will be safely stored in flash. Furthermore, it should also be expected that in order to accelerate writes but maintain the data safety condition, the SSDs will contain super capacitors to provide just enough power to flush the SSDs RAM buffer to flash in the event of a power loss condition.

Enterprise SSDs are normally provided in a number of different flavors to provide a wide cost per GB options balanced against write endurance.

Enterprise – read intensive

Read intensive SSDs are a bit of a marketing term. All SSDs will easily handle reads, but the name is referring to the lower write endurance. They will, however, provide the best cost per GB. These SSDs will often only have a write endurance of around 0.3-1 over a 5 year period **drive writes per day (DWPD)**. That is to say you should be able to write 400 GB a day to a 400 GB SSD and expect it to still be working in 5 years' time. If you write 800 GB a day to it, it will only be guaranteed to last 2.5 years. In general, for most Ceph workloads, these ranges of SSDs are normally deemed to not have enough write endurance.

Enterprise – general usage

General usage SSDs will normally provide 3-5 DWPD and are a good balance of cost and write endurance. For using in Ceph, they will normally be a good choice for a SSD-based OSD assuming that the workload on the Ceph cluster is not planned to be overly write heavy.

Enterprise – write intensive

Write intensive SSDs are the most expensive type; they will often offer write endurances up to and over 10 DWPD. They should be used for journals for spinning disks in Ceph clusters or also for SSD-only OSDs if very heavy write workloads are planned.

Currently, Ceph uses **filestore** as its method of storing objects on disks. The details of how and why filestore works is covered later in `Chapter 3`, *BlueStore*. For now, it's important to understand that due to the limitations in normal POSIX filesystems to be able to provide atomic transactions to the several pieces of data Ceph needs to write a journal is used. If no separate SSD is used for the journal, a separate partition is created for it. Every write that the OSD handles will first be written to the journal and then flushed to the main storage area on the disk. This is the main reason why using SSD for a journal for spinning disks is advised. The double write severely impacts spinning disk performance, which is mainly caused by the random nature of the disk heads moving between the journal and data areas.

Likewise, SSD OSD still requires a journal, and so it will experience approximately double the number of writes and thus provide half the client performance expected.

As can now be seen, not all models of SSDs are equal, and Ceph's requirements can make choosing the correct one a tough process. Fortunately, a quick test can be carried out to establish SSD's potential for use as a Ceph journal.

Memory

Official recommendations are for 1 GB of memory for every 1 TB of storage. In truth, there are a number of variables that lead to this recommendation, but suffice to say that you never want to find yourself where your OSDs are running low on memory and any excess memory will be used to improve performance.

Aside from the baseline memory usage of OSD, the main variable effecting memory usage is the number of PGs running on OSD. Although total data size does have an impact on memory usage, it is dwarfed by the effect of the number of PGs. A healthy cluster running within the recommendations of 200 PGs per OSD will probably use less than 2 GB of RAM per OSD. However, in a cluster where the number of PGs has been set higher against best practice, memory usage will be higher. It is also worth noting that when OSD is removed from a cluster, extra PGs will be placed on remaining OSDs to rebalance the cluster; this will also increase memory usage as well as the recovery operation itself. This spike in memory usage can sometimes be the cause of cascading failures if insufficient ram has been provisioned. A large swap partition on SSD should always be provisioned to reduce the risk of the Linux **out-of-memory** (**OOM**) killer randomly killing OSD processes in the event of a low memory situation.

As a minimum, look to provision around 2 GB per OSD + OS overheads, but this should be treated as the bare minimum and 4 GB per OSD would be recommended.

Depending on your workload and size of spinning disks being used for the Ceph OSDs, extra memory may be required to ensure that the operating system can sufficiently cache the directory entries and file nodes from the filesystem used to store the Ceph objects. This may have a bearing on the RAM you wish to configure your nodes with and is covered in more detail in the tuning section of the book.

Regardless of the configured memory size, ECC memory should be used at all times.

CPU

Ceph's official recommendations are for 1 GHz of CPU power per OSD. Unfortunately, in real life, it's not quite as simple as this. What the official recommendations don't point out is that a certain amount of CPU power is required per I/O, and it's not just a static figure. Thinking about it, this makes sense; the CPU is only used when there is something to be done. No I/O, no CPU is required. This, however, scales the other way, more I/O, more CPUs are required. The official recommendation is a good safe bet for spinning disk-based OSDs. An OSD node equipped with fast SSDs can often find itself consuming several times this recommendation. To complicate things further, the CPU requirements vary depending on I/O size as well with larger I/Os requiring more CPU.

If the OSD node starts to struggle for CPU resource, it can lead to OSDs to start timing out and get marked out from the cluster, often to rejoin several seconds later. This continual loss and recovery tends to place more strain on the already limited CPU resource causing cascading failures.

A good figure to aim for would be around 1-10 MHz per I/O, corresponding to 4 KB-4 MB I/Os, respectively. As always, testing should be carried out before going live to confirm that CPU requirements are met both in normal and stressed I/O loads.

Another aspect of CPU selection, which is key to determine performance in Ceph, is the clock speed of the cores. A large proportion of the I/O path in Ceph is single threaded and so a faster clocked core will run through this code path faster leading to lower latency. Due to the limited thermal design of most CPUs, there is often a trade-off of clock speed as the number of cores increases. High core count CPUs with high clock speeds also tend to be placed at the top of the pricing structure. Therefore, it is beneficial to understand your I/O and latency requirements to choose the best CPU.

A small experiment was done to find the effect of CPU clock speed against write latency. A Linux workstation running Ceph had its CPU clock manually adjusted using the userspace governor. The following results clearly show the benefit of high-clocked CPUs:

CPU MHz	4 KB write I/O	Average latency (microseconds)
1600	797	1250
2000	815	1222
2400	1161	857
2800	1227	812
3300	1320	755
4300	1548	644

If low latency and especially low write latency is important, then go for the highest clocked CPUs you can get, ideally at least higher than 3 GHz. This may require a compromise in SSD only nodes on how many cores are available and thus how many SSDs each node can support. For nodes with 12 spinning disks and SSD journals, single socket quad core processors make an excellent choice as they are often available with very high clock speeds and are very aggressively priced.

Where latency is not as important, for example, object workloads, look at entry-level processors with well-balanced core counts and clock speeds.

Another consideration around CPU and motherboard choice should be around the number of sockets. In Dual socket designs, the memory, disk controllers, and **network interface controllers (NICs)** are shared between the sockets. When data required by one CPU is required from a resource located on another CPU's socket, it must cross the interlink bus between the two CPUs. Modern CPUs have high-speed interconnects, but they do introduce some performance penalty and thought should be given to whether a single socket design is achievable. There are some options given in the tuning section on how to work around some of these possible performance penalties.

Disks

When choosing the disks to build a Ceph cluster with, there is always the temptation to go with the biggest disks you can, as the figures look great on paper. Unfortunately, in reality, this is often not a great choice. Although disks have dramatically increased in capacity over the past 20 years, their performance hasn't. First, ignore any sequential MBps figures, and you will never see them in enterprise workloads. There is always something making the I/O pattern nonsequential enough that it might as well be random. Second, remember these figures:

7.2k disks = 70-80 4k IOPS

10k disks = 120-150 4k IOPS

15k disks = You should be using SSDs

As a general rule, if you are designing a cluster that will offer active workloads rather than bulk inactive/archive storage. Design for the required **Input/Output Operations Per Second** (**IOPS**), not capacity. If your cluster will contain largely spinning disks with the intention of providing storage for an active workload, an increased number of smaller capacity disks are normally preferred over the use of larger disks. With the decrease in cost of SSD capacity, serious thought should be given to using them in your cluster, either as a cache tier or even for a full SSD cluster.

A thought should also be given to the use of SSDs as either journals with Ceph's filestore or for storing the DB and **write-ahead log** (**WAL**) when using **BlueStore**. Filestore performance is dramatically improved when using SSD journals and would not be recommended to be used without unless the cluster is designed to be used with very cold data.

Also, consider that the default replication level of 3 will mean that each client write I/O will generate at least 3x the I/O on the backend disks. In reality, due to the internal mechanisms in Ceph, this number in some instances will be nearer six times write amplification. If no SSD journals are to be used in the cluster, then this number might be nearer 12 times write amplification in the worst case scenarios.

Understand that although Ceph enables much more rapid recovery from a failed disk as every disk in the cluster will take part in the recovery. However, larger disks still pose a challenge, particularly when looking at having to recover from a node failure. In a cluster comprising 10 1 TB disks each 50% full, in the event of a disk failure, the remaining disks would have to recover 500 GB of data between them or around 55 GB each. At an average recovery speed of 20 MBps, recovery would be expected in around 45 minutes. A cluster with a hundred 1 TB disks would still only have to recover 500 GB of data, but this time, that task is shared between 99 disks. In theory for the larger cluster to recover from a single disk failure, it would take around four minutes. In reality, these recovery times will be higher as there are additional mechanisms at work, which increases recovery time. In smaller clusters, recovery times should be a key factor when selecting disk capacity.

Networking

The network is a key and often overlooked component in a Ceph cluster; a poorly designed network can often lead to a number of problems that manifest themselves in peculiar ways and make for a confusing troubleshooting session.

10G networking requirement

10G networking is strongly recommended for building a Ceph cluster, while 1G networking will work; latency will be pushing on the bounds of being unacceptable and will limit you to the size of nodes you can deploy. A thought should also be given to recovery; in the event of a disk or node failure, large amounts of data will need to be moved around the cluster. Not only will a 1G network be able to provide sufficient performance for this, but normal I/O traffic will be impacted. In the very worst of cases, this may lead to OSDs timing out causing cluster instabilities.

As mentioned, one of the main benefits of 10G networking is the lower latency. Quite often a cluster will never push enough traffic to make full use of the 10G bandwidth; however, the latency improvement is realized, no matter the load on the cluster. The round time trip for a 4k packet over a 10G network might take around 90 microseconds, and the same 4k packet over 1G networking will take over 1 milliseconds. In the tuning section of this book, you will learn that latency has a direct effect on the performance of a storage system, particularly when performing direct or synchronous I/O.

If your OSD node will come equipped with dual NICs, strongly look into a network design that allows you to use them active/active for both transmit and receive. It's wasteful to leave a 10G link in a passive state and will help to lower latency under load.

Network design

A good network design is an important step to bringing a Ceph cluster online. If your networking is handled by another team, make sure that they are included at all stages of the design as often an existing network will not be designed to handle Ceph's requirements, leading to both poor Ceph performance as well as impacting existing systems.

It's recommended that each Ceph node be connected via redundant links to two separate switches so that in the event of a switch failure, the Ceph node is still accessible. Stacking switches should be avoided if possible, as they can introduce single points of failure and in some cases are both required to be offline to carry out firmware upgrades.

If your Ceph cluster will be contained purely in one set of switches, feel free to skip this next section.

Traditional networks were mainly designed around a North-South access path, where clients at the North, access data through the network to servers at the South. If a server connected to an access switch needed to talk to another server connected to another access switch, the traffic would be routed through the core switch. Due to this access pattern, the access and aggregation layers that feed into the core layer were not designed to handle a lot of intraserver traffic, which is fine for the environment they were designed to support. Server-to-server traffic is named East-West traffic and is becoming more prevalent in the modern data center as applications become less isolated and require data from several other servers.

Ceph generates a lot of East-West traffic, not only from internal cluster replication traffic, but also from other servers consuming Ceph storage. In large environments, the traditional core, aggregation, and access layer design may struggle to cope as large amounts of traffic will be expected to be routed through the core switch. Faster switches can be obtained, and faster or more uplinks can be added; however, the underlying problem is that you are trying to run a scale-out storage system on a scale-up network design. Following image shows a typical network design with Core, Aggregation and Access layers. Typically only a single link from the access to the aggregation layer will be active.

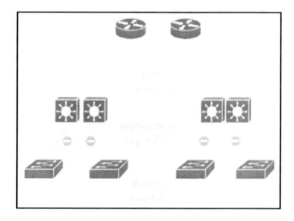

A design that is becoming very popular in data centers is leaf-spine design. This approach completely gets rid of the traditional model and instead replaces it with two layers of switches: the spine layer and the leaf layer. The core concept is that each leaf switch connects to every spine switch so that any leaf switch is only one hop anyway from any other leaf switch. This provides consistent hop latency and bandwidth. Following is an example of a leaf spine toplogy. Depending on failure domains you may wish to have single or multiple leaf switches per rack for redundancy.

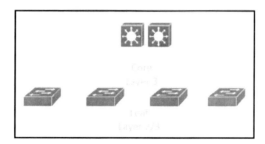

The leaf layer is where the servers connect into and is typically made up of a large number of 10G ports and a handful of 40G or faster uplink ports to connect into the spine layer.

The spine layer won't normally connect directly into servers, unless there are certain special requirements and will just serve as an aggregation point for all the leaf switches. The spine layer will often have higher port speeds to reduce any possible contention of the traffic coming out of the leaf switches.

Leaf spine networks are typically moving away from pure layer 2 topology, where layer 2 domain is terminated on the leaf switches and layer 3 routing is done between the leaf and spine layer. This is advised to be done using dynamic routing protocols, such as **Border Gateway Protocol** (BGP) or **Open Shortest Path First** (OSPF), to establish the routes across the fabric. This brings numerous advantages over large layer 2 networks. Spanning tree, which is typically used in layer 2 networks to stop switching loops, works by blocking an uplink, when using 40G uplinks; this is a lot of bandwidth to lose. When using dynamic routing protocols with a layer 3 design, **Equal-cost multi-path** (ECMP) routing can be used to fairly distribute data over all uplinks to maximize the available bandwidth. In the example of a leaf switch connected to two spine switches via a 40G uplink, there would be 80G of bandwidth available to any other leaf switch in the topology, no matter where it resides.

Some network designs take this even further and push the layer 3 boundary down to the servers by actually running these routing protocols on servers as well so that ECMP can be used to simplify the use of both NICs on the server in an active/active fashion. This is named **Routing on the Host**.

OSD node sizes

A common approach when designing nodes for use with Ceph is to pick a large capacity server, which contains large numbers of disks slots. In certain designs, this may be a good choice, but for most scenarios with Ceph, smaller nodes are more preferable. To decide on the number of disks each node in your Ceph cluster should contain, there are a number of things you should consider, some of the main considerations are listed as follows.

Failure domains

If your cluster will have less than 10 nodes, this is probably the most important point.

With legacy scale-up storage, the hardware is expected to be 100% reliable. All components are redundant, and the failure of a complete component such as a system board or disk JBOD would likely cause an outage. Therefore, there is no real knowledge of how such a failure might impact the operation of the system, just the hope that it doesn't happen! With Ceph, there is an underlying assumption that complete failure of a section of your infrastructure, be that a disk, node, or even rack should be considered as normal and should not make your cluster unavailable.

Let's take two Ceph clusters both comprising 240 disks. Cluster A comprises 20x12 disk nodes; Cluster B comprises 4x60 disk nodes. Now, let's take a scenario where for whatever reason a Ceph OSD node goes offline. It could be due to planned maintenance or unexpected failure, but that node is now down and any data on it is unavailable. Ceph is designed to mask this situation and will even recover from it whilst maintaining full data access.

In the case of cluster *A*, we have now lost 5% of our disks and in the event of a permanent loss would have to reconstruct 72 TB of data. Cluster *B* has lost 25% of its disks and would have to reconstruct 360 TB. The latter would severely impact the performance of the cluster, and in the case of data reconstruction, this period of degraded performance could last for many days.

It's clear that on smaller sized clusters, these very large dense nodes are not a good idea. A 10 Ceph node cluster is probably the minimum size if you want to reduce the impact of node failure, and so in the case of 60 drive JBODs, you would need a cluster that at minimum is measured in petabytes.

Price

One often cited reason for wanting to go with large dense nodes is to try and drive down the cost of the hardware purchase. This is often a false economy as dense nodes tend to require premium parts that often end up costing more per GB than less dense nodes.

For example, a 12 disk node may only require a single quad processor to provide enough CPU resource for OSDs. A 60 bay enclosure may require dual 10 core processors or greater, which are a lot more expensive per GHz provided. You may also need larger **Dual In-line Memory Modules (DIMMs)**, which demand a premium and perhaps even increased numbers of 10G or even 40G NICs.

The bulk of the cost of the hardware will be made up of the CPUs, memory, networking, and disks. As we have seen, all of these hardware resource requirements scale linearly with the number and size of disks. The only area that larger nodes may have an advantage in is requiring fewer motherboards and power supplies, which is not a large part of the overall cost.

Power supplies

Servers can be configured with either single or dual redundant power supplies. Traditional workloads normally demand dual power supplies to protect against downtime in the case of a power supply or feed failure. If your Ceph cluster is large enough, then you may be able to look into the possibility of running single PSUs in your OSD nodes and allow Ceph to provide the availability in case of a power failure. Consideration should be given to the benefits of running a single power supply versus the worst case situation where an entire feed goes offline at DC.

How to plan a successful Ceph implementation

In order to be certain your Ceph implementation will be succesfull, there are a number of rules you should follow:

- Use 10G networking as a minimum
- Research and test the correctly sized hardware you wish to use
- Don't use the nobarrier mount option
- Don't configure pools with size=2 or minsize=1
- Don't use consumer SSDs
- Don't use RAID controllers in writeback without battery protection
- Don't use configuration options you don't understand
- Implement some form of change management
- Do carry out power loss testing
- Do have an agreed backup and recovery plan

Understanding your requirements and how it relates to Ceph

As we have discussed, Ceph is not always the right choice for every storage requirement. Hopefully, this chapter has given you the knowledge to be able to help you identify your requirements and match them to Ceph's capabilities. Hopefully though, Ceph is a good fit for your use case and you can proceed with the project.

Care should be taken to understand the requirements of the project including the following:

- Who are the key stakeholders of the project, they will likely be the same people that will be able to detail how Ceph will be used.
- Collect details of what systems Ceph will need to interact with. If it becomes apparent, for example, that unsupported operating systems are expected to be used with Ceph, this needs to be flagged at an early stage.

Defining goals so that you can gauge if the project is a success

Every project should have a series of goals that can help identify if the project has been a success. Example goals may be:

- Cost no more than X
- Provide X IOPS or MBps of performance
- Survive certain failure scenarios
- Reduce ownership costs of storage by X

These goals will need to be revisited throughout the life of the project to make sure that it is on track.

Choosing your hardware

The infrastructure section of this chapter will have given you a good idea on the hardware requirements of Ceph and the theory behind selecting the correct hardware for the project. The second biggest cause of outages with a Ceph cluster is caused by poor hardware choices, making the right choices early on in the design stage crucial.

If possible, check with your hardware vendor to see if they have any reference designs, these are often certified by Red Hat and will take a lot of the hard work off your shoulders in trying to determine if your hardware choices are valid. You can also ask Red Hat or your chosen Ceph support vendor to validate your hardware; they will have had previous experience and will be able to guide you around any questions you may have.

Finally, if you are planning on deploying and running your Ceph cluster entirely in-house without any third-party involvement or support, consider reaching out to the Ceph community. The Ceph-users mailing list is participated in by individuals from vastly different backgrounds stretching right round the globe. There is a high chance that someone somewhere will be doing something similar to you and will be able to advise you on hardware choice.

Training yourself and your team to use Ceph

As with all technologies, it's essential that Ceph administrators receive some sort of training. Once the Ceph cluster goes live and becomes a business dependency, unexperienced administrators are a risk to stability. Depending on your reliance on third-party support, various levels of training may be required and may also determine if you look for a training course or self teach.

Running PoC to determine if Ceph has met the requirements

A **proof of concept** (PoC) cluster should be deployed to test the design and identify any issues early on before proceeding with full-scale hardware procurement. This should be treated as a decision point in the project; don't be afraid to revisit goals or start design from fresh if any serious issues are uncovered. If you have existing hardware of similar specifications, then it should be fine to use it in the proof of concept, but the aim should be to try and test hardware that is as similar as possible to what you intend to build the production cluster with, so as to be able to fully test the design.

As well as testing for stability, the PoC cluster should also be used to forecast if it looks likely that the goals you have set for the project will be met.

The proof of concept stage is also a good time to firm up your knowledge on Ceph, practice day-to-day operations and test out features. This will be of benefit further down the line. You should also take this opportunity to be as abusive as possible to your PoC cluster. Randomly pull out disks, power off nodes, and disconnect network cables. If designed correctly, Ceph should be able to withstand all of these events. Carrying out this testing now will give you the confidence to operate Ceph at larger scale where these events will happen and also help you understand how to troubleshoot them more easily if needed.

Following best practices to deploy your cluster

When deploying your cluster, attention should be paid to understanding the process rather than following guided examples. This will give you better knowledge of the various components that make up Ceph and should you encounter any errors during deployment or operation, you will be much better placed to solve them. The next chapter of this book goes into more detail on deployment of Ceph, including the use of orchestration tools.

Initially, it is recommended that the default options for both the operating system and Ceph are used. It is better to start from a known state should any issues arise during deployment and initial testing.

RADOS pools replication level should be left at the default of 3 and the minimum replication level of 2. This corresponds to the pool variables of `size` and `min_size`, respectively. Unless there is both a good understanding and reason for the impact of lowering these values, it would be unwise to change them. The replication size determines how many copies of data will be stored in the cluster, and the effects of lowering it should be obvious in terms of protection against data loss. Less understood is the effect of `min_size` in relation to data loss and is a common reason for it.

The `min_size` variable controls how many copies the cluster must write to acknowledge the write back to a client. A `min_size` of 2 means that the cluster must be able to write two copies of data; this can mean in a severely degraded scenario that write operations are blocked if the PG has only one remaining copy and will continue to do so until the PG is recovered to have two copies of the object. This is the reason that there may be a desire to decrease `min_size` to 1 so that in this event, cluster operations can still continue and if availability is more important than consistency, then this can be a valid decision. However, with a `min_size` of 1, data may be written to only one OSD and there is no guarantee that the number of desired copies will be met anytime soon. During that period, any component failure will likely result in loss of data written in the degraded state. If summary downtime is bad, data loss is typically worse and these two settings will probably have one of the biggest impacts on the probability of data loss.

Defining a change management process

The biggest cause of data loss and outages with a Ceph cluster is normally human error, whether it be by accidently running the wrong command or changing configuration options, which may have unintended consequences. These incidents will likely become more common as the number of people in the team administering Ceph grows. A good way of reducing the risk of human error causing service interruptions or data loss is to implement some form of change control. This is covered in the next chapter in more detail.

Creating a backup and recovery plan

Ceph is highly redundant and when properly designed should have no single point of failure and be resilient to many types of hardware failures. However, one in a million situations do occur and as we have also discussed, human error can be very unpredictable. In both cases, there is a chance that the Ceph cluster may enter a state where it is unavailable or data loss occurs. In many cases, it may be possible to recover some or all of the data and return the cluster to full operation. However, in all cases, a full backup and recovery plan should be discussed before putting any live data onto a Ceph cluster. Many businesses have gone out of business or lost faith from customers when it's revealed that not only has there been an extended period of downtime, but critical data has also been lost. It may be that as a result of discussion it is agreed that a backup and recovery plan is not required; this is fine. As long as risks and possible outcomes have been discussed and agreed, that is the important part.

Summary

In this chapter, you learned all the necessary steps to allow you to successfully plan and implement a Ceph project. You learned about the available hardware choices, how they relate to Ceph's requirements, and how they affect both Ceph's performance and reliability.

Finally, you will have awareness of the importance of the processes and procedures that should be in place to ensure a healthy operating environment for your Ceph cluster.

2
Deploying Ceph

Once you have planned your Ceph project and are ready to either deploy a test or production cluster, you will need to consider the method you wish to use to both deploy and maintain it. This chapter will demonstrate how to quickly deploy test environments for testing and development by the use of Vagrant. It will also explain the reasons why you might want to consider using an orchestration tool to deploy Ceph rather than using the supplied Ceph tools. As a popular orchestration tool, Ansible will be used to show how quickly and reliably a Ceph cluster can be deployed and the advantages that using it can bring.

In this chapter, you will learn about the following topics:

- Preparing a testing environment with Vagrant and VirtualBox
- Learning about the differences between `ceph-deploy` and orchestration tools
- The advantages of using orchestration tools
- Installing and using Ansible
- Configuring the Ceph Ansible modules
- Deploying a test cluster with Vagrant and Ansible
- Ideas around how to manage your Ceph configuration

Preparing your environment with Vagrant and VirtualBox

Although a test cluster can be deployed on any hardware or **virtual machine** (**VM**), for the purposes of this book, a combination of Vagrant and VirtualBox will be used. This will allow rapid provisioning of the VMs and ensure a consistent environment.

VirtualBox is a free and open source *type 2* (hosted) hypervisor currently being developed by Oracle. Performance and features may be lacking compared with high-end hypervisors, but its lightweight approach, and multi-OS support lends itself to be a prime candidate for testing.

Vagrant helps allow an environment that may comprise many machines to be created quickly and efficiently. It works with the concepts of boxes, which are predefined templates for use with hypervisors and its **Vagrantfile**, which defines the environment to be built. It supports multiple hypervisors and allows a Vagrantfile to be portable across them.

System requirements

In order to be able to run the Ceph environment described later in this chapter, it's important that your computer meets a number of following requirements to ensure that the VM can be provided with sufficient resources:

- An **operating system** (**OS**) compatible with Vagrant and VirtualBox; this includes Linux, macOS, and Windows
- 2 Core CPU
- 8 GB RAM
- Virtualization instructions enabled in the bios

Obtaining and installing VirtualBox

Visit the VirtualBox web site at `https://www.virtualbox.org`and download the package that is appropriate with the OS you are using.

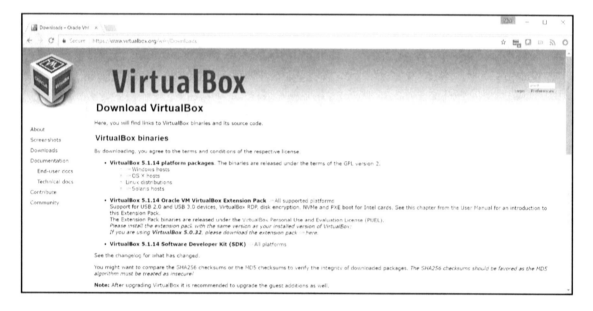

Setting up Vagrant

Perform the following steps in order to set up Vagrant:

1. Follow installation instructions from Vagrant's website `https://www.vagrantup.com/downloads.html` to get Vagrant installed on your chosen OS:

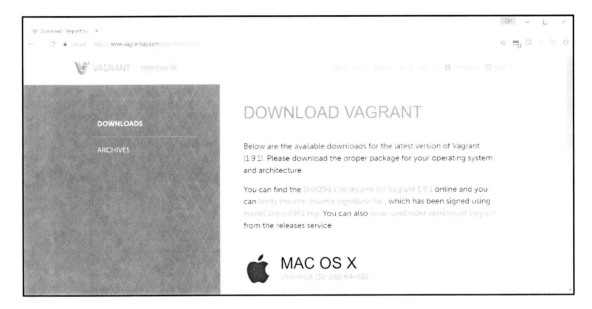

2. Create a new directory for your Vagrant project; for example, `ceph-ansible`.
3. Change to this directory and run the following commands:

```
C:\Users\nfisk\vagrant>cd ceph

C:\Users\nfisk\vagrant\ceph>
```

```
vagrant plugin install vagrant-hostmanager
```

The preceding command gives the following output:

```
Installing the 'vagrant-hostmanager' plugin. This can take a few minutes...
Fetching: vagrant-hostmanager-1.8.5.gem (100%)
Installed the plugin 'vagrant-hostmanager (1.8.5)'!
```

```
vagrant box add bento/ubuntu-16.04
```

The preceding command gives the following output:

```
==> box: Loading metadata for box 'bento/ubuntu-16.04'
    box: URL: https://atlas.hashicorp.com/bento/ubuntu-16.04
This box can work with multiple providers! The providers that it
can work with are listed below. Please review the list and choose
the provider you will be working with.

1) parallels
2) virtualbox
3) vmware_desktop

Enter your choice: 2
==> box: Adding box 'bento/ubuntu-16.04' (v2.3.1) for provider: virtualbox
    box: Downloading: https://atlas.hashicorp.com/bento/boxes/ubuntu-16.04/versions/2.3.1/providers/virtualbox.box
    box: Progress: 100% (Rate: 5257k/s, Estimated time remaining: --:--:--)
==> box: Successfully added box 'bento/ubuntu-16.04' (v2.3.1) for 'virtualbox'!
```

Now create an empty file named `Vagrantfile` and place the following into it:

```
nodes = [
  { :hostname => 'ansible', :ip => '192.168.0.40', :box => 'xenial64'
  },
  { :hostname => 'mon1', :ip => '192.168.0.41', :box => 'xenial64' },
  { :hostname => 'mon2', :ip => '192.168.0.42', :box => 'xenial64' },
  { :hostname => 'mon3', :ip => '192.168.0.43', :box => 'xenial64' },
  { :hostname => 'osd1', :ip => '192.168.0.51', :box => 'xenial64',
  :ram => 1024, :osd => 'yes' },
  { :hostname => 'osd2', :ip => '192.168.0.52', :box => 'xenial64',
  :ram => 1024, :osd => 'yes' },
  { :hostname => 'osd3', :ip => '192.168.0.53', :box => 'xenial64',
  :ram => 1024, :osd => 'yes' }
]

Vagrant.configure("2") do |config|
  nodes.each do |node|
    config.vm.define node[:hostname] do |nodeconfig|
      nodeconfig.vm.box = "bento/ubuntu-16.04"
      nodeconfig.vm.hostname = node[:hostname]
      nodeconfig.vm.network :private_network, ip: node[:ip]

      memory = node[:ram] ? node[:ram] : 512;
      nodeconfig.vm.provider :virtualbox do |vb|
        vb.customize [
          "modifyvm", :id,
          "--memory", memory.to_s,
        ]
        if node[:osd] == "yes"
          vb.customize [ "createhd", "--filename", "disk_osd-#
          {node[:hostname]}", "--size", "10000" ]
          vb.customize [ "storageattach", :id, "--storagectl", "SATA
```

```
        Controller", "--port", 3, "--device", 0, "--type", "hdd",
        "--medium", "disk_osd-#{node[:hostname]}.vdi" ]
      end
    end
  end
  config.hostmanager.enabled = true
  config.hostmanager.manage_guest = true
  end
end
```

Just in case if you encounter error in this step, you need to disable Hyper-V.

Run `vagrant up` to bring up the VMs defined in `Vagrantfile`:

```
Bringing machine 'ansible' up with 'virtualbox' provider...
Bringing machine 'mon1' up with 'virtualbox' provider...
Bringing machine 'mon2' up with 'virtualbox' provider...
Bringing machine 'mon3' up with 'virtualbox' provider...
Bringing machine 'osd1' up with 'virtualbox' provider...
Bringing machine 'osd2' up with 'virtualbox' provider...
Bringing machine 'osd3' up with 'virtualbox' provider...
==> ansible: Importing base box 'bento/ubuntu-16.04'...
==> ansible: Matching MAC address for NAT networking...
==> ansible: Checking if box 'bento/ubuntu-16.04' is up to date...
==> ansible: Setting the name of the VM: ceph_ansible_1486503043550_56998
==> ansible: Clearing any previously set network interfaces...
==> ansible: Preparing network interfaces based on configuration...
    ansible: Adapter 1: nat
    ansible: Adapter 2: hostonly
==> ansible: Forwarding ports...
    ansible: 22 (guest) => 2222 (host) (adapter 1)
==> ansible: Running 'pre-boot' VM customizations...
==> ansible: Booting VM...
==> ansible: Waiting for machine to boot. This may take a few minutes...
```

Now let's connect to the `ansible` VM using `ssh`:

```
vagrant ssh ansible
```

The preceding command gives the following output:

```
`ssh` executable not found in any directories in the %PATH% variable. Is an
SSH client installed? Try installing Cygwin, MinGW or Git, all of which
contain an SSH client. Or use your favorite SSH client with the following
authentication information shown below:

Host: 127.0.0.1
Port: 2200
Username: vagrant
```

 If you are running Vagrant on Windows, the `ssh` command will inform you that you need to use an SSH client of your choice and provide the details to use it.

PuTTY would be a good suggestion for an SSH client. On Linux, the command will connect you straight onto the VM.

The username and password are both `vagrant`. After logging in, you should find yourself sitting at the Bash shell of the `ansible` VM:

```
login as: vagrant
vagrant@127.0.0.1's password:
Welcome to Ubuntu 16.04.1 LTS (GNU/Linux 4.4.0-51-generic x86_64)

 * Documentation:  https://help.ubuntu.com
 * Management:      https://landscape.canonical.com
 * Support:         https://ubuntu.com/advantage

0 packages can be updated.
0 updates are security updates.

vagrant@ansible:~$
```

Simply type `exit` to return to your host machine.

Congratulations! You have just deployed three servers for using as Ceph monitors, three servers for using as Ceph OSDs, and an Ansible server. `Vagrantfile` could have also contained extra steps to execute commands on the servers to configure them, but for now, let's shut down the servers using the following command; we can bring them back up for when needed by the examples later in this chapter:

```
vagrant destroy --force
```

The ceph-deploy tool

`ceph-deploy` is the official tool to deploy **Ceph clusters**. It works on the principle of having an admin node with SSH access (without password) to all machines in your Ceph cluster; it also holds a copy of the Ceph configuration file. Every time you carry out a deployment action, it uses SSH to connect to your Ceph nodes to carry out the necessary steps. Although the `ceph-deploy` tool is an entirely supported method, which will leave you with a perfectly functioning Ceph cluster, ongoing management of Ceph will not be as easy as desired. Larger scale Ceph clusters will also cause a lot of management overheads if `ceph-deploy` is to be used. For this reason, it is recommended that `ceph-deploy` is limited to test or small-scale production clusters, although as you will see, an orchestration tool allows the rapid deployment of Ceph and is probably better suited for test environments where you might need to continually build new Ceph clusters.

Orchestration

One solution to making the installation and management of Ceph easier is to use an orchestration tool. There are several tools available, such as Puppet, Chef, Salt, and Ansible, all of which have Ceph modules available. If you are already using an orchestration tool in your environment, then it would be recommended that you stick to using that tool. For the purposes of this book, Ansible will be used; this is for a number of reasons:

- It's the favored deployment method of Red Hat, who are the owners of both the Ceph and Ansible projects
- It has a well-developed and mature set of Ceph roles and playbooks
- Ansible tends to be easier to learn if you have never used an orchestration tool before
- It doesn't require a central server to be set up, which means demonstrations are more focused on using the tool rather than installing it

All tools follow the same principle of where you provide them with an inventory of hosts and a set of tasks to be carried out on the hosts. These tasks often reference variables that allows customization of the task at runtime. Orchestration tools are designed to be run on a schedule so that if for any reason the state or configuration of a host changes, it will be correctly changed back to the intended state during the next run.

Another advantage of using orchestration tools is documentation. Although they are not a replacement for good documentation, the fact that they clearly describe your environment including roles and configuration options, means that your environment starts to become self-documenting. If you ensure that any installations or changes are carried out via your orchestration tool, then the configuration file of the orchestration tool will clearly describe the current state of your environment. If this is combined with something like a git repository to store the orchestration configuration, you have the makings of a change control system. This is covered in more detail later in this chapter. The only disadvantages are around the extra time it takes to carry out the initial setup and configuration of the tool.

So, using an orchestration tool, not only do you get a faster and less error-prone deployment, you also get documentation and change management for free. If you haven't got the hint by now, this is something you should really be looking at.

Ansible

As mentioned, Ansible will be the orchestration tool of choice for this book, let's look at it in a bit more detail.

Ansible is an agentless orchestration tool written in Python, which uses SSH to carry out configuration tasks on remote nodes. It was first released in 2012 and has gained widespread adoption, and it is known for its ease of adoption and low learning curve. Red Hat purchased the commercial company Ansible, Inc. in 2015 and so has a very well-developed and close-knit integration for deploying Ceph.

Files named **playbooks** are used in Ansible to describe a list of commands, actions, and configurations to carry out on specified hosts or groups of hosts and are stored in a YAML file format. Instead of having large unmanageable playbooks, Ansible roles can be created that allow a playbook to contain a single task, which may then carry out a number of tasks associated with the role.

The use of SSH to connect to remote nodes and execute the playbooks means that it is very lightweight and does not require either an agent or a centralized server.

For testing Ansible also integrates well with Vagrant, an Ansible playbook can be specified as part of the Vagrant provisioning configuration and will automatically generate an inventory file from the VM's Vagrant created and run the playbook once the servers have booted. This allows a Ceph cluster including OS to be deployed via just a single command.

Installing Ansible

Bring your Vagrant environment back up that you created earlier on and SSH onto the Ansible server. For this example, only `ansible`, `mon1`, and `osd1` will be needed, as follows:

```
vagrant up ansible mon1 osd1
```

Add the Ansible `ppa`, as follows:

```
$ sudo apt-add-repository ppa:ansible/ansible
```

The preceding command gives the following output:

```
Ansible is a radically simple IT automation platform that makes your applications and systems easie
r to deploy. Avoid writing scripts or custom code to deploy and update your applications- automate i
n a language that approaches plain English, using SSH, with no agents to install on remote systems.

http://ansible.com/
 More info: https://launchpad.net/~ansible/+archive/ubuntu/ansible
Press [ENTER] to continue or ctrl-c to cancel adding it

gpg: keyring '/tmp/tmpt5a6qdao/secring.gpg' created
gpg: keyring '/tmp/tmpt5a6qdao/pubring.gpg' created
gpg: requesting key 7BB9C367 from hkp server keyserver.ubuntu.com
gpg: /tmp/tmpt5a6qdao/trustdb.gpg: trustdb created
gpg: key 7BB9C367: public key "Launchpad PPA for Ansible, Inc." imported
gpg: Total number processed: 1
gpg:               imported: 1  (RSA: 1)
OK
```

Update **Advanced Package Tool** (**APT**) sources and install Ansible:

```
$ sudo apt-get update && sudo apt-get install ansible -y
```

The preceding command gives the following output:

```
Setting up libyaml-0-2:amd64 (0.1.6-3) ...
Setting up python-markupsafe (0.23-2build2) ...
Setting up python-jinja2 (2.8-1) ...
Setting up python-yaml (3.11-3build1) ...
Setting up python-crypto (2.6.1-6build1) ...
Setting up python-six (1.10.0-3) ...
Setting up python-ecdsa (0.13-2) ...
Setting up python-paramiko (1.16.0-1) ...
Setting up python-httplib2 (0.9.1+dfsg-1) ...
Setting up python-pkg-resources (20.7.0-1) ...
Setting up python-setuptools (20.7.0-1) ...
Setting up sshpass (1.05-1) ...
Setting up ansible (2.2.1.0-1ppa~xenial) ...
Processing triggers for libc-bin (2.23-0ubuntu4) ...
vagrant@ansible:~$
```

Creating your inventory file

The Ansible inventory file is used by Ansible to reference all known hosts and to which group they belong. A group is defined by placing its name in square brackets, groups can be nested inside other groups by the use of the children definition.

Before we add hosts to the inventory file, we first need to configure the remote nodes for SSH (without password); otherwise, we will have to enter a password every time Ansible tries to connect to a remote machine.

Generate an SSH key as follows:

```
$ ssh-keygen
```

The preceding command gives the following output:

```
vagrant@ansible:~$ ssh-keygen
Generating public/private rsa key pair.
Enter file in which to save the key (/home/vagrant/.ssh/id_rsa):
Enter passphrase (empty for no passphrase):
Enter same passphrase again:
Your identification has been saved in /home/vagrant/.ssh/id_rsa.
Your public key has been saved in /home/vagrant/.ssh/id_rsa.pub.
The key fingerprint is:
SHA256:mdvKrx6ZG88AKQsPnaFpjKlPb8pmmnfqDiQPv4OQnpw vagrant@ansible
The key's randomart image is:
+---[RSA 2048]----+
|                 |
|       .         |
|  + + o . o      |
|=oB + o S        |
|*= + o . =       |
|*.* o   B .      |
|.E=oo  . O       |
|oBO*.  .*o+      |
+-----[SHA256]----+
```

Copy the key to the remote hosts:

```
$ ssh-copy-id mon1
```

The preceding command gives the following output:

```
vagrant@ansible:~$ ssh-copy-id mon1
/usr/bin/ssh-copy-id: INFO: Source of key(s) to be installed: "/home/vagrant/.ssh/id_rsa.pub"
The authenticity of host 'mon1 (192.168.0.41)' can't be established.
ECDSA key fingerprint is SHA256:RI5/3ep65qXeDkZSACi/rN0hBxiLrBxMvcyk9CfLkyg.
Are you sure you want to continue connecting (yes/no)? yes
/usr/bin/ssh-copy-id: INFO: attempting to log in with the new key(s), to filter out any that are alr
eady installed
/usr/bin/ssh-copy-id: INFO: 1 key(s) remain to be installed -- if you are prompted now it is to inst
all the new keys
vagrant@mon1's password:

Number of key(s) added: 1

Now try logging into the machine, with:   "ssh 'mon1'"
and check to make sure that only the key(s) you wanted were added.
```

This will need to be repeated for each host. Normally, you would include this step in your Vagrant provisioning stage, but it is useful to carry out these tasks manually the first couple of times so that an understanding of the process is learned.

Now try logging into the machine using `ssh mon1`:

```
vagrant@ansible:~$ ssh mon1
Welcome to Ubuntu 16.04.1 LTS (GNU/Linux 4.4.0-51-generic x86_64)

 * Documentation:  https://help.ubuntu.com
 * Management:    . https://landscape.canonical.com
 * Support:         https://ubuntu.com/advantage

0 packages can be updated.
0 updates are security updates.

vagrant@mon1:~$
```

Type `exit` to return to the Ansible VM.

Now, let's create the Ansible inventory file.

Edit the file named `hosts in /etc/ansible`:

```
$ sudo nano /etc/ansible/hosts
```

Create two groups named `osds` and `mons` and finally a third group named `ceph`. This third group will contain the `osds` and `mons` groups as children.

Enter a list of your hosts under the correct group, as follows:

```
[mons]
mon1
mon2
mon3

[osds]
osd1
osd2
osd3

[ceph:children]
mons
osds
```

Variables

Most playbooks and roles will make use of variables; these variables can be overridden in several ways. The simplest way is to create files in the `host_vars` and `groups_vars` folders, these allow you to override variables either based on the host or group membership, respectively. For this, perform the following steps:

1. Create a directory `/etc/ansible/group_vars`.
2. Create a file in `group_vars` named `mons`. Add the following in `mons`:

   ```
   a_variable: "foo"
   ```

3. Create a file in `group_vars` named `osds`. Add the following in `osds`:

   ```
   a_variable: "bar"
   ```

Variables follow a precedence order; you can also create an `all` file, which will apply to all groups. However, a variable of the same name that is in a more specific matching group will override it. The **Ceph Ansible modules** make use of this to allow you to have a set of default variables and then also allow you to specify different values for the specific roles.

Testing

To test that Ansible is working correctly and that we can successfully connect and run commands remotely, let's use the Ansible `ping` command to check one of our hosts. Note that this is not like a network ping, Ansible `ping` confirms that it can communicate via SSH and execute commands remotely:

```
$ ansible mon1 -m ping
```

The preceding command gives the following output:

```
vagrant@ansible:~$ ansible mon1 -m ping
mon1 | SUCCESS => {
    "changed": false,
    "ping": "pong"
}
vagrant@ansible:~$
```

Excellent, that worked, now let's run a simple command remotely to demonstrate the power of Ansible. The following command will retrieve the current running kernel version on the specified remote node:

```
$ ansible mon1 -a 'uname -r'
```

This is the desired result:

```
vagrant@ansible:~$ ansible mon1 -a 'uname -r'
mon1 | SUCCESS | rc=0 >>
4.4.0-51-generic

vagrant@ansible:~$
```

A very simple playbook

To demonstrate how playbooks work, the following example will show a small playbook that also makes use of the variables we configured earlier:

```
- hosts: mon1 osd1
tasks:
- name: Echo Variables
debug: msg="I am a {{ a_variable }}"
```

Now run the playbook. Note the command to run a playbook that differs from running ad hoc Ansible commands:

```
$ ansible-playbook /etc/ansible/playbook.yml
```

The preceding command gives the following output:

```
vagrant@ansible:~$ ansible-playbook /etc/ansible/playbook.yml

PLAY [mon1 osd1] ***************************************************************

TASK [setup] ******************************************************************
ok: [mon1]
ok: [osd1]

TASK [Echo Variables] *********************************************************
ok: [mon1] => {
    "msg": "I am a foo"
}
ok: [osd1] => {
    "msg": "I am a bar"
}

PLAY RECAP ********************************************************************
mon1                       : ok=2    changed=0    unreachable=0    failed=0
osd1                       : ok=2    changed=0    unreachable=0    failed=0

vagrant@ansible:~$
```

The output shows the playbook being executed on both mon1 and osd1 as they are in groups, which are children of the parent group ceph. Also, note how the output is different between the two servers as they are picking up the variables that you set earlier in the group_vars directory.

Finally, the last couple of lines show the overall run status of the playbook run. You can now destroy your Vagrant environment again, ready for the next section:

```
vagrant destroy --force
```

This concludes the introduction to Ansible, but it is not a complete guide. It's recommended that you should explore other resources to gain a more in-depth knowledge of Ansible before using it in a production environment.

Adding the Ceph Ansible modules

We can use `git` to clone the Ceph Ansible repository:

```
git clone https://github.com/ceph/ceph-ansible.git

sudo cp -a ceph-ansible/* /etc/ansible/
```

The preceding commands gives the following output:

```
vagrant@ansible:~$ git clone https://github.com/ceph/ceph-ansible.git
Cloning into 'ceph-ansible'...
remote: Counting objects: 13875, done.
remote: Compressing objects: 100% (69/69), done.
remote: Total 13875 (delta 32), reused 0 (delta 0), pack-reused 13802
Receiving objects: 100% (13875/13875), 2.29 MiB | 1.94 MiB/s, done.
Resolving deltas: 100% (9234/9234), done.
Checking connectivity... done.
vagrant@ansible:~$ sudo cp -a ceph-ansible/* /etc/ansible/
vagrant@ansible:~$
```

Let's also explore some of the key folders in the git repository:

- `group_vars`: We've already covered what lives in here and will explore the possible configuration options in more detail later.
- `infrastructure-playbooks`: This directory contains prewritten playbooks to carry out some standard tasks, such as deploying cluster or adding OSDs to an existing one. The comments at the top of the playbooks give a good idea of what they do.
- `roles`: This directory contains all the roles that make up the Ceph Ansible modules. You will see that there is a role for each Ceph component, these are what are called via the playbooks to install, configure and maintain Ceph.

In order to be able to deploy a Ceph cluster with Ansible a number of key variables need to be set in the `group_vars` directory. The following variables either are required to set or are advised to be changed from their defaults. For the remaining variables, it is suggested that you read the comments in the variable files.

The following are the key variables from `global`:

```
#mon_group_name: mons
#osd_group_name: osds
#rgw_group_name: rgws
#mds_group_name: mdss
#nfs_group_name: nfss
...
#iscsi_group_name: iscsigws
```

These control what group name the modules use to identify the types of Ceph hosts. If you will be using Ansible in a wider setting, it might be advisable to prepend `ceph-` to the start to make it clear that these groups are related to Ceph:

```
#ceph_origin: 'upstream' # or 'distro' or 'local'
```

Set to `upstream` to use the packages generated by the Ceph team, or `distro` for packages generated by your distribution maintainer. Setting to `upstream` is recommended if you want to be able to upgrade Ceph independently of your distribution.

By default a fsid will be generated for your cluster and stored in a file where it can be referenced again:

```
#fsid: "{{ cluster_uuid.stdout }}"
#generate_fsid: true
```

You shouldn't need to touch this unless you want control over the fsid or you wish to hard code the fsid in the group variable file.

```
#monitor_interface: interface
#monitor_address: 0.0.0.0
```

One of these should be specified. If you are using a variable in group_vars then you probably want to use the `monitor_interface`, which is the interface name as seen by the OS, as they will probably be the same across all `mons` groups. Otherwise if you specify the `monitor_address` in `host_vars`, you can specify the IP of the interface, which obviously will be different across your three or more `mons` groups.

```
#ceph_conf_overrides: {}
```

Not every Ceph variable is directly managed by Ansible, but the preceding variable is provided to allow you to pass any extra variables through to the `ceph.conf` file and its corresponding sections. An example of how this would look is (notice the indentation):

```
ceph_conf_overrides:
  global:
```

```
    variable1: value
  mon:
    variable2: value
  osd:
    variable3: value
```

Key variables from OSD variable file:

```
  #copy_admin_key: false
```

If you want to be able to manage your cluster from your OSD nodes instead of just your monitors, set this to `true`, which will copy the admin key to your OSD nodes:

```
  #devices: [] #osd_auto_discovery: false #journal_collocation:
  false #raw_multi_journal: false #raw_journal_devices: []
```

These are probably the most crucial set of variables in the whole configuration of Ansible. They control what disks get used as OSDs and how the journals are placed. You can either manually specify the devices that you wish to use as OSDs or you can use auto discovery. The examples in this book will use the static device configuration.

The `journal_collocation` variable sets whether you want to store the journal on the same disk as the OSD data; a separate partition will be created for it.

`raw_journal_devices` allows you to specify the devices you wish to use for journals. Quite often a single SSD will be a journal for several OSDs, in this case, enable `raw_multi_journal` and simply specify the journal device multiple times, no partition numbers are needed if you want Ansible to instruct `ceph-disk` to create them for you.

These are the main variables that you should need to consider. It is recommended that you read the comments in the variable files to see if there are any others you may need to modify for your environment.

Deploying a test cluster with Ansible

There are several examples on the Internet which contain a fully configured Vagrantfile and associated Ansible playbooks which allows you to bring up a fully functional Ceph environment with just one command. As handy as this may be it doesn't help to learn how to correctly configure and use the Ceph Ansible modules as you would if you were deploying a Ceph cluster on real hardware in a production environment. As such, this book will guide you through configuring Ansible from the scratch, although running on Vagrant provisioned servers.

At this point your Vagrant environment should be up and running, and Ansible should be able to connect to all six of your Ceph servers. You should also have a cloned copy of the Ceph Ansible module:

1. Create a file called `/etc/ansible/group_vars/ceph`:

   ```
   ceph_origin: 'upstream'
   ceph_stable: true # use ceph stable branch
   ceph_stable_key: https://download.ceph.com/keys/release.asc
   ceph_stable_release: jewel # ceph stable release
   ceph_stable_repo: "http://download.ceph.com/debian-{{
   ceph_stable_release }}"monitor_interface: enp0s8 #Check ifconfig
   public_network: 192.168.0.0/24
   journal_size: 1024
   ```

2. Create a file called `/etc/ansible/group_vars/osds`:

   ```
   devices:
     - /dev/sdb
   journal_collocation: true
   ```

3. Create a `fetch` folder and change the owner to the `vagrant` user:

   ```
   sudo mkdir /etc/ansible/fetch
   sudo chown vagrant /etc/ansible/fetch
   ```

4. Run the Ceph cluster deployment playbook:

   ```
   cd /etc/ansible
   sudo mv site.yml.sample site.yml
   ansible-playbook -K site.yml
   ```

The `K` parameter tells Ansible that it should ask you for the `sudo` password.

Now sit back and watch Ansible deploy your cluster:

```
PLAY RECAP *********************************************************************
mon1                       : ok=57    changed=15    unreachable=0    failed=0
mon2                       : ok=51    changed=12    unreachable=0    failed=0
mon3                       : ok=51    changed=12    unreachable=0    failed=0
osd1                       : ok=59    changed=11    unreachable=0    failed=0
osd2                       : ok=57    changed=11    unreachable=0    failed=0
osd3                       : ok=57    changed=11    unreachable=0    failed=0
```

Once done, assuming Ansible completed without errors, SSH into `mon1` and run the following code. If Ansible did encounter errors, scroll up and look for the part which errored, the error text should give you a clue as to why it failed.

```
vagrant@mon1:~$ sudo ceph -s:
```

```
vagrant@ansible:/etc/ansible$ ssh mon1
Welcome to Ubuntu 16.04.1 LTS (GNU/Linux 4.4.0-51-generic x86_64)

 * Documentation:  https://help.ubuntu.com
 * Management:     https://landscape.canonical.com
 * Support:        https://ubuntu.com/advantage

93 packages can be updated.
28 updates are security updates.


Last login: Tue Feb  7 22:08:42 2017 from 192.168.0.40
vagrant@mon1:~$ sudo ceph -s
    cluster d9f58afd-3e62-4493-ba80-0356290b3d9f
     health HEALTH_OK
     monmap e1: 3 mons at {mon1=192.168.0.41:6789/0,mon2=192.168.0.42:6789/0,mon3=192.168.0.43:6789/0}
            election epoch 6, quorum 0,1,2 mon1,mon2,mon3
     osdmap e8: 3 osds: 3 up, 3 in
            flags sortbitwise,require_jewel_osds
      pgmap v15: 64 pgs, 1 pools, 0 bytes data, 0 objects
            100 MB used, 26794 MB / 26894 MB avail
                  64 active+clean
```

And that concludes the deployment of a fully functional Ceph cluster via Ansible.

If you want to be able to stop the Vagrant Ceph cluster without losing your work so far, you can run the following command:

```
vagrant suspend
```

This will pause all the VMs in their current state.

The following command will power the VMs on and resume running at the state you left them:

```
vagrant resume
```

Change and configuration management

If you deploy your infrastructure with an orchestration tool such as Ansible, managing the Ansible playbooks becomes important. As we have seen Ansible allows you to rapidly deploy both the initial Ceph cluster but also configuration updates further down the line. It must be appreciated that this power can also have devastating effects if incorrect configuration or operations are deployed. By implementing some form of configuration management, Ceph administrators will clearly be able to see what changes have been made to the Ansible playbooks before running them.

A recommended approach would be to store your Ceph Ansible configuration in a git repository, this will allow you to track changes and gives the ability to implement some form of change control either by monitoring git commits or by forcing people to submit merge requests into the master branch.

Summary

In this chapter you will have learnt about the various deployment methods of Ceph that are available and the differences between them. You will now also have a basic understanding of how Ansible works and how to deploy a Ceph cluster with it. It would be advisable at this point to continue investigating and practicing deployment and configuration of Ceph with Ansible, so that you are confident to use it in production environments. The rest of this book will also make several assumptions that you have fully understood the contents of this chapter in order to manipulate the configuration of Ceph.

3
BlueStore

In this chapter, you will learn about BlueStore, the new object store in Ceph designed to replace the existing filestore. Its increased performance and enhanced feature set are designed to allow Ceph to continue to grow and provide a resilient high-performance distributed storage system for the future.

You will learn the following topics:

- What is BlueStore?
- The limitations with filestore
- What problems BlueStore overcomes
- The components of BlueStore and how it works
- How to deploy BlueStore OSDs

What is BlueStore?

BlueStore is a Ceph object store that is primarily designed to address the limitations of filestore, which, as of the **Kraken** release, is the current object store. Initially, a new object store was being developed to replace filestore, with a highly original name of **NewStore**. NewStore was a combination of **RocksDB**, a key value store to store metadata and a standard **portable operating system interface** (**POSIX**) filesystem for the actual objects. However, it quickly became apparent that using a POSIX filesystem still introduced high overheads, which was one of the key reasons from trying to move away from filestore.

Thus, BlueStore was born; using raw block devices in combination with RocksDB, a number of problems were solved that had stunted NewStore. The name *BlueStore* was a reflection of the combination of the words *Block* and *NewStore*:

Block+NewStore=BlewStore=BlueStore

BlueStore is designed to remove the double write penalty associated with filestore and improve performance. Also, with the ability to now have more control over the way objects are stored on disk, additional features, such as checksums and compression, can be implemented.

Why was it needed?

The current object store in Ceph, Filestore, has a number of limitations which have started to limit the scale at which Ceph can operate and features that it can offer. Following are some of the main reasons why Bluestore was needed.

Ceph's requirements

An object in Ceph along with its data also has certain metadata associated with it, and it's crucial that both the data and metadata are updated atomically. If either of this metadata or data is updated without the other, the whole consistency model of Ceph is at risk. To ensure that these updates occur atomically, they need to be carried out in a single transaction.

Filestore limitations

Filestore was originally designed as an object store to enable developers to test Ceph on their local machines. Due to its stability, it quickly became the standard object store and found itself in use in production clusters throughout the world.

Initially, the thought behind filestore was that the upcoming **B-tree file system (btrfs)**, which offered transaction support, would allow Ceph to offload the atomic requirements to btrfs. Transactions allow an application to send a series of requests to btrfs and only receive acknowledgement once all have been committed to stable storage. Without a transaction support, if there is an interruption halfway through a Ceph write operation, either the data or metadata could be missing or one out of sync with the other.

Unfortunately, the reliance on btrfs to solve these problems turned out to be a false hope, and several limitations were discovered. btrfs can still be used with filestore, but there are numerous known issues that can affect the stability of Ceph.

In the end, it turned out that **XFS** was the best choice to use with filestore, but XFS had the major limitation that it didn't support transactions, meaning that there was no way for Ceph to guarantee atomicity of its writes. The solution to this was the write-ahead journal. All writes including data and metadata would first be written into a journal, residing on a raw block device. Once the filesystem containing the data and metadata confirmed that all data had been safely flushed to disk, the journal entries could be flushed. A beneficial side effect of this is that when using a SSD to hold the journal for a spinning disk, it acts like a write back cache, lowering the latency of writes to the speed of the SSD. However, if the filestore journal resides on the same storage device as the data partition, then throughput will be at least halved. In the case of spinning disk OSDs, this can lead to very poor performance as the disk heads are constantly moving between two areas of the disks, even for sequential operations. Although filestore on SSD-based OSDs don't suffer nearly the same performance penalty, their throughput is still effectively halved due to double the amount of data required to be written. In either case, this loss of performance is very undesirable and in the case of flash, also wears the device faster, requiring more expensive write endurance flash. The following diagram shows how Filestore and its journal interacts with a block device, you can see that all data operations have to go through the Filestore journal and the filesystems journal.

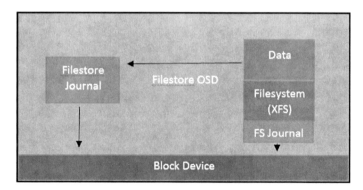

Additional challenges with filestore were around trying to control the actions of the underlying POSIX filesystem to perform and behave in a way that Ceph required. Large amounts of work has been done over the years by filesystem developers to try and make filesystems intelligent and to predict how an application might submit I/O. In the case of Ceph, a lot of these optimizations interfere with what it's trying to instruct the filesystem to do, requiring more work around and complexity.

Object metadata is stored in combinations of filesystem attributes named **Extended Attributes (XATTRs)** and in a **LevelDB** key value store, which also resides on the OSD disk. LevelDB was chosen at the time of filestore's creation rather than RocksDB, as RocksDB was not available and LevelDB suited a lot of Ceph's requirements.

Ceph is designed to scale to petabytes of data and store billions of objects. However, due to limitations around the number of files you can reasonably store in a directory, further workarounds to help limit this were introduced. Objects are stored in a hierarchy of hashed directory names; when the number of files in one of these folders reaches the set limit, the directory is split into a further level and the objects moved. However, there is a trade-off to improving the speed of object enumeration, when these directory splits occur they impact performance as the objects are moved into the correct directories. On larger disks, the increased number of directories puts additional pressure on the VFS cache and can lead to additional performance penalties for infrequently accessed objects.

As this book will cover in the performance tuning chapter, a major performance bottleneck in filestore is when XFS has to start looking up **inodes** and directory entries as they are not currently cached in RAM. For scenarios where there are a large number of objects stored per OSD, there is currently no real solution to this problem, and it's quite common to observe that the Ceph cluster gradually starts to slow down as it fills up.

Moving away from storing objects on a POSIX filesystem is really the only way to solve most of these problems.

Why is BlueStore the solution?

BlueStore was designed to address these limitations. From the development of NewStore, it was obvious that trying to use a POSIX filesystem as the underlying storage layer in any approach would introduce a number of issues that were also present in filestore. In order for Ceph to be able to get the guarantees, it not only needed from the storage but also without the overheads of a filesystem, Ceph needed to have direct block level access to the storage devices. By storing metadata in RocksDB and the actual object data directly on block devices, Ceph can leverage much better control over the underlying storage and at the same time, also provide better performance.

How BlueStore works

The following diagram shows how Bluestore interacts with a block device. Unlike filestore, data is directly written to the block device and metadata operations are handled by RocksDB.

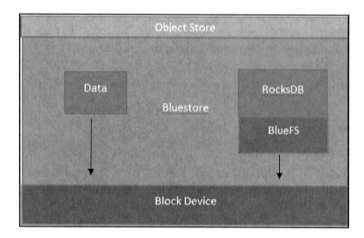

RocksDB

RocksDB is a high-performance key value store, which was originally forked from LevelDB, but after development, Facebook went on to offer significant performance improvements suited for multiprocessor servers with low latency storage devices. It has also had numerous feature enhancements, some of which are used in BlueStore.

RocksDB is used to store metadata about the stored objects, which was previously handled by a combination of LevelDB and XATTRs in filestore.

A feature of RocksDB, which BlueStore takes advantage of, is the ability to store the WAL on a faster storage device, which can help to lower latency of RocksDB operations. This also hopefully improves Ceph's performance, particularly for smaller I/Os. This gives a number of possible storage layout configurations, where the WAL, DB, and data can be placed on different storage devices. Three examples are given here:

- WAL, DB, and data all on spinning disk
- WAL and DB on SSD, data on spinning disk
- WAL on NVMe, DB on SSD, and data on spinning disk

Deferred writes

Unlike in filestore where every write is written in its entirely to both the journal and finally to disk, in BlueStore, the data part of the write in most cases is written directly to the block device. This removes the double write penalty and on pure spinning disk OSDs dramatically improves performance. However, as mentioned previously, this double write has a side effect of decreasing write latency when the spinning disks are combined with SSD journals. BlueStore can also use flash-based storage devices to lower write latency by deferring writes, first writing data into the RocksDB WAL and then later flushing these entries to disk. Unlike filestore, not every write is written into the WAL, configuration parameters determine the I/O size cut-off as to what writes are deferred. The configuration parameter is shown here:

```
bluestore_prefer_deferred_size
```

This controls the size of I/Os that will be written to the WAL first. For spinning disks, this defaults to 32 KB, and SSDs by default do not defer writes. If write latency is important and your SSD is sufficiently fast, then by increasing this value, you can increase the size of I/Os that you wish to defer to WAL.

BlueFS

Although the main driver of BlueStore was not to use an underlying filesystem, BlueStore still needs a method to store RocksDB and the data on the OSD disk. BlueFS was developed, which is an extremely cut down filesystem that provides just the minimal set of features that BlueStore requires. It also means that it has been designed to operate in a dependable manner for the slim set of operations that Ceph submits. It also removes the overhead of the double journal write impact that would be present when using a standard POSIX filesystem.

How to use BlueStore

To create a BlueStore OSD, you can use ceph-disk that fully supports creating BlueStore OSDs with either the RocksDB data and WAL collocated or stored on separate disks. The operation is similar to when creating a filestore OSD except instead of specifying a device for use as the filestore journal, you specify devices for the RocksDB data. As previously mentioned, you can separate the DB and WAL parts of RocksDB if you so wish:

```
ceph-disk prepare --bluestore /dev/sda --block.wal /dev/sdb --block.db
/dev/sdb
```

The preceding code assumes that your data disk is /dev/sda. For this example, assume a spinning disk and you have a faster device such as SSD as /dev/sdb. Ceph-disk would create two partitions on the data disk: one for storing the actual Ceph objects and another small XFS partition for storing details about the OSD. It would also create two partitions for SSD for the DB and WAL. You can create multiple OSDs sharing the same SSD for DB and WAL without fear of overwriting previous OSDs; ceph-disk is smart enough to create new partitions without having to specify them.

However, as we discovered in Chapter 2, *Deploying Ceph* using a proper deployment tool for your Ceph cluster helps to reduce deployment time and ensures consistent configuration across the cluster. Although the Ceph Ansible modules also support deploying BlueStore OSDs, at the time of publication of this book, it did not currently support deploying separate DB and WAL partitions. For the basis of demonstrating BlueStore, we will use ceph-disk to non-disruptively manually upgrade our test cluster's OSDs from filestore to BlueStore.

Upgrading an OSD in your test cluster

Make sure that your Ceph cluster is in full health by checking with the ceph -s command. We will be upgrading OSD by first removing it from the cluster and then letting Ceph recover the data onto the new BlueStore OSD. By taking advantage of this hot maintenance capability in Ceph, you can repeat this procedure across all the OSDs in your cluster.

In this example, we will remove osd.2, which is residing on the /dev/sdb disk on the OSD node, by performing the following steps:

1. Use the following command:

   ```
   sudo ceph osd out 2
   ```

   The preceding command gives the following output:

   ```
   vagrant@mon1:~$ sudo ceph osd out 2
   marked out osd.2.
   ```

2. Log into the OSD node that contains the OSD you wish to recreate. We will stop the service and unmount the XFS partition:

   ```
   systemctl stop ceph-osd@2
   umount /dev/sdb1
   ```

3. Go back to one of your monitors and now remove the OSD using the following commands:

```
sudo ceph osd crush remove osd.2
```

The preceding command gives the following output:

```
vagrant@mon1:~$ sudo ceph osd crush remove osd.2
removed item id 2 name 'osd.2' from crush map
```

```
sudo ceph auth del osd.2
```

The preceding command gives the following output:

```
vagrant@mon1:~$ sudo ceph auth del osd.2
updated
```

```
sudo ceph osd rm osd.2
```

The preceding command gives the following output:

```
vagrant@mon1:~$ sudo ceph osd rm osd.2
removed osd.2
```

4. Check the status of your Ceph cluster with the `ceph -s` command. You should now see that the OSD has been removed. Once recovery has completed, you can now recreate the disk as a BlueStore OSD.

5. Go back to your OSD node and run the following `ceph-disk` command to wipe the partition details from the disk:

```
sudo ceph-disk zap /dev/sdb
```

The preceding command gives the following output:

```
vagrant@osd3:~$ sudo ceph-disk zap /dev/sdb
Caution: invalid backup GPT header, but valid main header; regenerating
backup header from main header.

Warning! Main and backup partition tables differ! Use the 'c' and 'e' options
on the recovery & transformation menu to examine the two tables.

Warning! One or more CRCs don't match. You should repair the disk!

***************************************************************************
Caution: Found protective or hybrid MBR and corrupt GPT. Using GPT, but disk
verification and recovery are STRONGLY recommended.
***************************************************************************
GPT data structures destroyed! You may now partition the disk using fdisk or
other utilities.
Creating new GPT entries.
The operation has completed successfully.
```

6. Now issue the `ceph-disk` command to create the `bluestore` OSD. In this example, we will not be storing the WAL and DB on separate disks, so we do not need to specify those options:

```
ceph-disk prepare --bluestore /dev/sdb
```

The preceding command gives the following output:

```
vagrant@osd3:~$ sudo ceph-disk prepare --bluestore /dev/sdb
Setting name!
partNum is 0
REALLY setting name!
The operation has completed successfully.
Setting name!
partNum is 1
REALLY setting name!
The operation has completed successfully.
The operation has completed successfully.
meta-data=/dev/sdb1          isize=2048   agcount=4, agsize=6400 blks
         =                   sectsz=512   attr=2, projid32bit=1
         =                   crc=1        finobt=1, sparse=0
data     =                   bsize=4096   blocks=25600, imaxpct=25
         =                   sunit=0      swidth=0 blks
naming   =version 2          bsize=4096   ascii-ci=0 ftype=1
log      =internal log       bsize=4096   blocks=864, version=2
         =                   sectsz=512   sunit=0 blks, lazy-count=1
realtime =none               extsz=4096   blocks=0, rtextents=0
The operation has completed successfully.
```

7. And finally activate OSD:

```
ceph-disk activate /dev/sdb1
```

Returning to our monitor node, we can now run another `ceph -s` and see that a new OSD has been created and data is starting to be backfilled to it.

As you can see, the overall procedure is very simple and is identical to the steps required to replace a failed disk.

Summary

In this chapter, you learned about the new object store in Ceph named BlueStore. Hopefully, you have a better understanding of why it was needed and the limitations in the existing filestore design. You should also have a basic understanding of the inner workings of BlueStore and feel confident in how to upgrade your OSDs to BlueStore.

4
Erasure Coding for Better Storage Efficiency

Ceph's default replication level provides excellent protection against data loss by storing three copies of your data on different OSDs. The chance of losing all three disks that contain the same objects, within the period that it takes Ceph to rebuild from a failed disk, is verging on the extreme edge of probability. However, storing three copies of data vastly increases both the purchase cost of the hardware and also associated operational costs such as power and cooling. Furthermore, storing copies also means that for every client write, the backend storage must write three times the amount of data. In some scenarios, either of these drawbacks may mean that Ceph is not a viable option.

Erasure codes are designed to offer a solution. Much like how RAID 5 and 6 offer increased usable storage capacity over RAID 1, erasure coding allows Ceph to provide more usable storage from the same raw capacity. However, also like the parity-based RAID levels, erasure coding brings its own set of disadvantages.

In this chapter you will learn the following:

- What is erasure coding and how does it work?
- Details around Ceph's implementation of erasure coding
- How to create and tune an erasure-coded RADOS pool
- A look into the future features of erasure coding with the Ceph Kraken release

What is erasure coding?

Erasure coding allows Ceph to achieve either greater usable storage capacity or increase resilience to disk failure for the same number of disks versus the standard replica method. Erasure coding achieves this by splitting up the object into a number of parts and then also calculating a type of **cyclic redundancy check** (**CRC**), the erasure code, and then storing the results in one or more extra parts. Each part is then stored on a separate OSD. These parts are referred to as K and M chunks, where K refers to the number of data shards and M refers to the number of erasure code shards. As in RAID, these can often be expressed in the form **K+M**, or *4+2*, for example.

In the event of an OSD failure which contains an object's shard which is one of the calculated erasure codes, data is read from the remaining OSDs that store data with no impact. However, in the event of an OSD failure which contains the data shards of an object, Ceph can use the erasure codes to mathematically recreate the data from a combination of the remaining data and erasure code shards.

K+M

The more erasure code shards you have, the more OSD failures you can tolerate and still successfully read data. Likewise, the ratio of K to M shards each object is split into has a direct effect on the percentage of raw storage that is required for each object.

A *3+1* configuration will give you 75% usable capacity but only allows for a single OSD failure, and so would not be recommended. In comparison, a three-way replica pool only gives you 33% usable capacity.

4+2 configurations would give you 66% usable capacity and allows for two OSD failures. This is probably a good configuration for most people to use.

At the other end of the scale, *18+2* would give you 90% usable capacity and still allows for two OSD failures. On the surface this sounds like an ideal option, but the greater total number of shards comes at a cost. A higher number of total shards has a negative impact on performance and also an increased CPU demand. The same 4 MB object that would be stored as a whole single object in a replicated pool would now be split into 20x200 KB chunks, which have to be tracked and written to 20 different OSDs. Spinning disks will exhibit faster bandwidth, measured in MBps with larger I/O sizes, but bandwidth drastically tails off at smaller I/O sizes. These smaller shards will generate a large amount of small I/O and cause additional load on some clusters.

Also, it's important not to forget that these shards need to be spread across different hosts according to the CRUSH map rules: no shard belonging to the same object can be stored on the same host as another shard from the same object. Some clusters may not have a sufficient number of hosts to satisfy this requirement.

Reading back from these high chunk pools is also a problem. Unlike in a replica pool where Ceph can read just the requested data from any offset in an object, in an erasure pool, all shards from all OSDs have to be read before the read request can be satisfied. In the *18+2* example, this can massively amplify the amount of required disk read ops and average latency will increase as a result. This behavior is a side effect which tends to only cause a performance impact with pools that use a large number of shards. A *4+2* configuration in some instances will get a performance gain compared to a replica pool, from the result of splitting an object into shards. As the data is effectively striped over a number of OSDs, each OSD has to write less data and there are no secondary and tertiary replicas to write.

How does erasure coding work in Ceph?

As with replication, Ceph has a concept of a primary OSD, which also exists when using erasure-coded pools. The primary OSD has the responsibility of communicating with the client, calculating the erasure shards, and sending them out to the remaining OSDs in the PG set. This is illustrated in the following diagram:

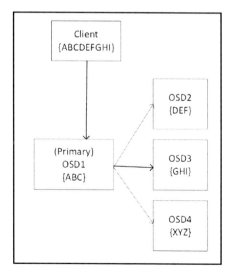

If an OSD in the set is down, the primary OSD can use the remaining data and erasure shards to reconstruct the data, before sending it back to the client. During read operations, the primary OSD requests all OSDs in the PG set to send their shards. The primary OSD uses data from the data shards to construct the requested data, and the erasure shards are discarded. There is a fast read option that can be enabled on erasure pools, which allows the primary OSD to reconstruct the data from erasure shards if they return quicker than data shards. This can help to lower average latency at the cost of a slightly higher CPU usage. The following diagram shows how Ceph reads from an erasure-coded pool:

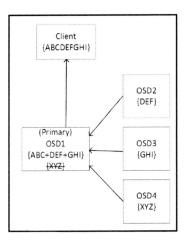

The following diagram shows how Ceph reads from an erasure pool when one of the data shards is unavailable. Data is reconstructed by reversing the erasure algorithm using the remaining data and erasure shards:

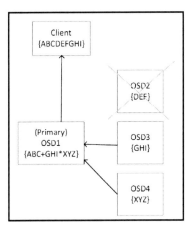

Algorithms and profiles

There are a number of different erasure plugins you can use to create your erasure-coded pool.

Jerasure

The default erasure plugin in Ceph is the **Jerasure** plugin, which is a highly optimized open source erasure coding library. The library has a number of different techniques that can be used to calculate the erasure codes. The default is **Reed-Solomon** and provides good performance on modern processors which can accelerate the instructions that the technique uses. **Cauchy** is another technique in the library; it is a good alternative to Reed- Solomon and tends to perform slightly better. As always, benchmarks should be conducted before storing any production data on an erasure-coded pool to identify which technique best suits your workload.

There are also a number of other techniques that can be used which all have a fixed number of M shards. If you are intending on only having two M shards, then they can be a good candidate as their fixed size means that optimizations are possible, lending to increased performance.

In general, the Jerasure profile should be preferred in most cases unless another profile has a major advantage, as it offers well-balanced performance and is well-tested.

ISA

The **ISA library** is designed to work with Intel processors and offers enhanced performance. It too supports both Reed-Solomon and Cauchy techniques.

LRC

One of the disadvantages of using erasure coding in a distributed storage system is that recovery can be very intensive on networking between hosts. As each shard is stored on a separate host, recovery operations require multiple hosts to participate in the process. When the CRUSH topology spans multiple racks, this can put pressure on the inter-rack networking links. The **Locally Repairable erasure Code** (LRC) erasure plugin adds an additional parity shard, which is local to each OSD node. This allows recovery operations to remain local to the node where an OSD has failed and remove the need for nodes to receive data from all other remaining shard-holding nodes.

However, the addition of these local recovery codes does impact the amount of usable storage for a given number of disks. In the event of multiple disk failures, the LRC plugin has to resort to using global recovery, as would happen with the Jerasure plugin.

SHEC

The **Shingled Erasure Coding (SHEC)** profile is designed with similar goals to the LRC plugin, in that it reduces the networking requirements during recovery. However, instead of creating extra parity shards on each node, SHEC shingles the shards across OSDs in an overlapping fashion. The shingle part of the plugin name represents the way the data distribution resembles shingled tiles on a roof of a house. By overlapping the parity shards across OSDs, the SHEC plugin reduces recovery resource requirements for both single and multiple disk failures.

Where can I use erasure coding?

Since the **Firefly** release of Ceph in 2014, there has been the ability to create a RADOS pool using erasure coding. There is one major thing that you should be aware of: the erasure coding support in RADOS does not allow an object to be partially updated. You can write to an object in an erasure pool, read it back, and even overwrite it whole, but you cannot update a partial section of it. This means that erasure-coded pools can't be used for RBD and CephFS workloads and are limited to providing pure object storage either via the RADOS gateway or applications written to use librados.

The solution at the time was to use the cache tiering ability which was released around the same time, to act as a layer above an erasure-coded pool so that RBD could be used. In theory this was a great idea; in practice, performance was extremely poor. Every time an object was required to be written to, the whole object first had to be promoted into the cache tier. This act of promotion probably also meant that another object somewhere in the cache pool was evicted. Finally, the object now in the cache tier could be written to. This whole process of constantly reading and writing data between the two pools meant that performance was unacceptable, unless a very high percentage of the data was idle.

During the development cycle of the Kraken release, an initial implementation for support for direct overwrites on an erasure-coded pool was introduced. As of the final Kraken release, support is marked as experimental and is expected to be marked as stable in the following release. Testing of this feature will be covered later in this chapter.

Creating an erasure-coded pool

Let's bring our test cluster up again and switch into **superuser** mode in Linux, so we don't have to keep prepending `sudo` to our commands.

Erasure-coded pools are controlled by the use of erasure profiles; these controls how many shards each object is broken up into including the split between data and erasure shards. The profiles also include configuration to determine what erasure code plugin is used to calculate the hashes.

The following plugins are available to use:

- Jerasure
- ISA
- LRC
- SHEC

To see a list of the erasure profiles, run the following command:

```
# ceph osd erasure-code-profile ls
```

You can see there is a `default` profile in a fresh installation of Ceph:

```
vagrant@mon1:~$ sudo ceph osd erasure-code-profile ls
default
```

Let's see what configuration options it contains using the following command:

```
# ceph osd erasure-code-profile get default
```

The `default` profile specifies that it will use the Jerasure plugin with the Reed-Solomon error-correcting codes and will split objects into 2 data shards and 1 erasure shard:

```
vagrant@mon1:~$ sudo ceph osd erasure-code-profile get default
k=2
m=1
plugin=jerasure
technique=reed_sol_van
```

This is almost perfect for our test cluster; however, for the purpose of this exercise, we will create a new profile using the following commands:

```
# ceph osd erasure-code-profile set example_profile k=2 m=1
plugin=jerasure technique=reed_sol_van
# ceph osd erasure-code-profile ls
```

You can see our new `example_profile` has been created:

```
vagrant@mon1:~$ sudo ceph osd erasure-code-profile ls
default
example_profile
```

Now, let's create our erasure-coded pool with this profile:

```
# ceph osd pool create ecpool 128 128 erasure example_profile
```

The preceding command gives the following output:

```
vagrant@mon1:~$ sudo ceph osd pool create ecpool 128 128 erasure example_profile
pool 'ecpool' created
```

The preceding command instructs Ceph to create a new pool called `ecpool` with `128` PGs. It should be an erasure-coded pool and should use the `example_profile` we previously created.

Let's create an object with a small text string inside it and then prove the data has been stored by reading it back:

```
# echo "I am test data for a test object" | rados --pool
ecpool put Test1 -
# rados --pool ecpool get Test1 -
```

That proves that the erasure-coded pool is working, but it's hardly the most exciting of discoveries:

```
root@mon1:/home/vagrant# echo "I am test data for a test object" | rados --pool ecpool put Test1 -
root@mon1:/home/vagrant# rados --pool ecpool get Test1 -
I am test data for a test object
```

Let's have a look to see if we can see what's happening at a lower level.

First, find out what PG is holding the object we just created:

```
# ceph osd map ecpool Test1
```

The result of the preceding command tells us that the object is stored in PG 3.40 on OSDs 1, 2, and 0 in this example Ceph cluster. That's pretty obvious as we only have three OSDs, but in larger clusters that is a very useful piece of information:

```
root@mon1:/home/vagrant# ceph osd map ecpool Test1
osdmap e114 pool 'ecpool' (3) object 'Test1' -> pg 3.ae48bdc0 (3.40) -> up ([1,2,0], p1) acting ([1,2,0
], p1)
```

> The PGs will likely be different on your test cluster, so make sure the PG folder structure matches the output of the preceding ceph osd map command.

We can now look at the folder structure of the OSDs and see how the object has been split using the following commands:

```
ls -l /var/lib/ceph/osd/ceph-2/current/1.40s0_head/
```

The preceding command gives the following output:

```
root@osd1:/home/vagrant# ls -l /var/lib/ceph/osd/ceph-0/current/3.40s2_head/
total 4
-rw-r--r-- 1 ceph ceph    0 Feb 12 19:53 __head_00000040__3_ffffffffffffffff_2
-rw-r--r-- 1 ceph ceph 2048 Feb 12 19:56 Test1__head_AE48BDC0__3_ffffffffffffffff_2
```

```
# ls -l /var/lib/ceph/osd/ceph-1/current/1.40s1_head/
```

The preceding command gives the following output:

```
root@osd2:/home/vagrant# ls -l /var/lib/ceph/osd/ceph-2/current/3.40s1_head/
total 4
-rw-r--r-- 1 ceph ceph    0 Feb 12 19:53 __head_00000040__3_ffffffffffffffff_1
-rw-r--r-- 1 ceph ceph 2048 Feb 12 19:56 Test1__head_AE48BDC0__3_ffffffffffffffff_1
```

```
# ls -l /var/lib/ceph/osd/ceph-0/current/1.40s2_head/
total 4
```

The preceding command gives the following output:

```
root@osd3:/home/vagrant# ls -l /var/lib/ceph/osd/ceph-1/current/3.40s0_head/
total 4
-rw-r--r-- 1 ceph ceph    0 Feb 12 19:53 __head_00000040__3_ffffffffffffffff_0
-rw-r--r-- 1 ceph ceph 2048 Feb 12 19:56 Test1__head_AE48BDC0__3_ffffffffffffffff_0
```

Notice how the PG directory names have been appended with the shard number and replicated pools just have the PG number as their directory name. If you examine the contents of the object files, you will see our text string that we entered into the object when we created it. However, due to the small size of the text string, Ceph has padded out the second shard with null characters and the erasure shard, hence it will contain the same as the first. You can repeat this example with a new object containing larger amounts of text to see how Ceph splits the text into the shards and calculates the erasure code.

Overwrites on erasure code pools with Kraken

Introduced for the first time in the Kraken release of Ceph as an experimental feature was the ability to allow partial overwrites on erasure-coded pools. **Partial overwrite** support allows RBD volumes to be created on erasure-coded pools, making better use of the raw capacity of the Ceph cluster.

In parity RAID, where a write request doesn't span the entire stripe, a read-modify-write operation is required. This is needed as the modified data chunks will mean the parity chunk is now incorrect. The RAID controller has to read all the current chunks in the stripe, modify them in memory, calculate the new parity chunk, and finally write this back out to the disk.

Ceph is also required to perform this read-modify-write operation, however the distributed model of Ceph increases the complexity of this operation. When the primary OSD for a PG receives a write request that will partially overwrite an existing object, it first works out which shards will not be fully modified by the request and contacts the relevant OSDs to request a copy of these shards. The primary OSD then combines these received shards with the new data and calculates the erasure shards. Finally, the modified shards are sent out to the respective OSDs to be committed. This entire operation needs to conform to the other consistency requirements Ceph enforces; this entails the use of temporary objects on the OSD, should a condition arise that Ceph needs to roll back a write operation.

This partial overwrite operation, as can be expected, has a performance impact. In general, the smaller the write I/Os, the greater the apparent impact. The performance impact is a result of the I/O path now being longer, requiring more disk I/Os, and extra network hops. However, it should be noted that due to the striping effect of erasure-coded pools, in the scenario where full stripe writes occur, performance will normally exceed that of a replication-based pool. This is simply down to there being less write amplification due to the effect of striping. If the performance of an erasure pool is not suitable, consider placing it behind a cache tier made up of a replicated pool.

Despite partial overwrite support coming to erasure-coded pools in Ceph, not every operation is supported. In order to store RBD data on an erasure-coded pool, a replicated pool is still required to hold key metadata about the RBD. This configuration is enabled by using the -data-pool option with the **rbd utility**. Partial overwrite is also not recommended to be used with filestore. Filestore lacks several features that partial overwrites on erasure-coded pools use; without these features, extremely poor performance is experienced.

Demonstration

This feature requires the Kraken release or newer of Ceph. If you have deployed your test cluster with the Ansible and the configuration provided, you will be running Ceph Jewel release. The following steps show how to use Ansible to perform a rolling upgrade of your cluster to the Kraken release. We will also enable options to enable experimental options such as BlueStore and support for partial overwrites on erasure-coded pools.

Edit your group_vars/ceph variable file and change the release version from Jewel to Kraken.

Also, add the following:

```
ceph_conf_overrides:
  global:
    enable_experimental_unrecoverable_data_corrupting_features:
    "debug_white_box_testing_ec_overwrites bluestore"

And to correct a small bug when using Ansible to deploy Ceph Kraken, add
debian_ceph_packages:
  - ceph
  - ceph-common
  - ceph-fuse
```

To the bottom of the file, run the following Ansible playbook:

```
ansible-playbook -K infrastructure-playbooks/rolling_update.yml
```

The preceding command gives the following output:

```
vagrant@ansible:/etc/ansible$ ansible-playbook -K infrastructure-playbooks/rolling_update.yml
SUDO password:
[DEPRECATION WARNING]: docker is kept for backwards compatibility but usage is discouraged. The module
documentation details page may explain more about this rationale..
This feature will be removed in a
future release. Deprecation warnings can be disabled by setting deprecation_warnings=False in
ansible.cfg.
Are you sure you want to upgrade the cluster? [no]: yes
```

Ansible will prompt you to make sure that you want to carry out the upgrade. Once you confirm by entering `yes`, the upgrade process will begin.

Once Ansible has finished, all the stages should be successful, as shown in the following screenshot:

```
PLAY RECAP ***********************************************************************
localhost                  : ok=1    changed=0    unreachable=0    failed=0
mon1                       : ok=73   changed=13   unreachable=0    failed=0
mon2                       : ok=68   changed=7    unreachable=0    failed=0
mon3                       : ok=68   changed=7    unreachable=0    failed=0
osd1                       : ok=69   changed=9    unreachable=0    failed=0
osd2                       : ok=69   changed=9    unreachable=0    failed=0
osd3                       : ok=69   changed=9    unreachable=0    failed=0
```

Your cluster has now been upgraded to Kraken and can be confirmed by running `ceph -v` on one of your VMs running Ceph:

```
vagrant@mon1:~$ ceph -v
ceph version 11.2.0 (f223e27eeb35991352ebc1f67423d4ebc252adb7)
```

As a result of enabling the experimental options in the configuration file, every time you now run a Ceph command, you will be presented with the following warning:

```
vagrant@mon1:~$ sudo ceph -s
2017-02-10 20:56:29.825996 7f6f18fc9700 -1 WARNING: the following dangerous and experimental features are enabled: bluestor
e,debug_white_box_testing_ec_overwrites
2017-02-10 20:56:29.831159 7f6f18fc9700 -1 WARNING: the following dangerous and experimental features are enabled: bluestor
e,debug_white_box_testing_ec_overwrites
    cluster d9f58afd-3e62-4493-ba80-0356290b3d9f
     health HEALTH_WARN
            all OSDs are running kraken or later but the 'require_kraken_osds' osdmap flag is not set
     monmap e2: 3 mons at {mon1=192.168.0.41:6789/0,mon2=192.168.0.42:6789/0,mon3=192.168.0.43:6789/0}
            election epoch 46, quorum 0,1,2 mon1,mon2,mon3
        mgr active: mon1 standbys: mon2, mon3
     osdmap e74: 3 osds: 3 up, 3 in
            flags sortbitwise,require_jewel_osds
      pgmap v600: 64 pgs, 1 pools, 3920 bytes data, 2 objects
            107 MB used, 26787 MB / 26894 MB avail
                  64 active+clean
```

This is designed as a safety warning to stop you running these options in a live environment, as they may cause irreversible data loss. As we are doing this on a test cluster, it is fine to ignore, but it should be a stark warning not to run this anywhere near live data.

The next command that is required to be run is to enable the experimental flag, which allows partial overwrites on erasure-coded pools:

```
ceph osd pool get ecpool debug_white_box_testing_ec_overwrites
true
```

 Do not run this on production clusters.

Double check you still have your erasure pool called `ecpool` and the default `rbd` pool:

```
# ceph osd lspools
0 rbd,1 ecpool,
```

Now, create `rbd`. Notice that the actual RBD header object still has to live on a replica pool, but by providing an additional parameter, we can tell Ceph to store data for this RBD on an erasure-coded pool:

```
rbd create Test_On_EC --data-pool=ecpool --size=1G
```

The command should return without error and you now have an erasure-coded backed RBD image. You should now be able to use this image with any **librbd application**.

 Partial overwrites on erasure pools require BlueStore to operate efficiently. Whilst filestore will work, performance will be extremely poor.

Troubleshooting the 2147483647 error

This small section is included within the erasure coding chapter rather than the troubleshooting section of this book, as it's commonly seen with erasure-coded pools and so is very relevant to this chapter. An example of this error is shown in the following screenshot, when running the `ceph health detail` command:

```
pg 2.7a is creating+incomplete, acting [0,2,1,2147483647] (reducing pool broken_ecpool min_size from 4
may help; search ceph.com/docs for 'incomplete')
pg 2.79 is creating+incomplete, acting [1,0,2,2147483647] (reducing pool broken_ecpool min_size from 4
may help; search ceph.com/docs for 'incomplete')
pg 2.78 is creating+incomplete, acting [1,0,2147483647,2] (reducing pool broken_ecpool min_size from 4
may help; search ceph.com/docs for 'incomplete')
pg 2.7f is creating+incomplete, acting [0,2,1,2147483647] (reducing pool broken_ecpool min_size from 4
may help; search ceph.com/docs for 'incomplete')
```

If you see 2147483647 listed as one of the OSDs for an erasure-coded pool, this normally means that CRUSH was unable to find a sufficient number of OSDs to complete the PG peering process. This is normally due to the number of K+M shards being larger than the number of hosts in the CRUSH topology. However, in some cases this error can still occur even when the number of hosts is equal to or greater than the number of shards. In this scenario it's important to understand how CRUSH picks OSDs as candidates for data placement. When CRUSH is used to find a candidate OSD for a PG, it applies the CRUSH map to find an appropriate location in the CRUSH topology. If the result comes back as the same as a previously selected OSD, Ceph will retry to generate another mapping by passing slightly different values into the CRUSH algorithm. In some cases, if there is a similar number of hosts to the number of erasure shards, CRUSH may run out of attempts before it can suitably find the correct OSD mappings for all the shards. Newer versions of Ceph have mostly fixed these problems by increasing the CRUSH tunable `choose_total_tries`.

Reproducing the problem

In order to aid understanding of the problem in more detail, the following steps will demonstrate how to create an erasure-coded profile that will require more shards than our three node cluster can support.

Firstly, like earlier in the chapter, create a new erasure profile but modify the K/M parameters to be k=3 and m=1:

```
$ ceph osd erasure-code-profile set broken_profile k=3 m=1
plugin=jerasure technique=reed_sol_van
```

Now, create a pool with it:

```
$ ceph osd pool create broken_ecpool 128 128 erasure broken_profile
```

The preceding command gives the following result:

```
vagrant@mon1:~$ sudo ceph osd pool create broken_ecpool 128 128 erasure broken_profile
2017-02-12 19:25:55.660243 7f3c6b74e700 -1 WARNING: the following dangerous and experimental features a
re enabled: bluestore,debug_white_box_testing_ec_overwrites
2017-02-12 19:25:55.671201 7f3c6b74e700 -1 WARNING: the following dangerous and experimental features a
re enabled: bluestore,debug_white_box_testing_ec_overwrites
pool 'broken_ecpool' created
```

If we look at the output from ceph -s, we will see that the PGs for this new pool are stuck in the creating state:

```
    cluster d9f58afd-3e62-4493-ba80-0356290b3d9f
     health HEALTH_ERR
            128 pgs are stuck inactive for more than 300 seconds
            128 pgs incomplete
            128 pgs stuck inactive
            128 pgs stuck unclean
            all OSDs are running kraken or later but the 'require_kraken_osds' osdmap flag is not set
     monmap e2: 3 mons at {mon1=192.168.0.41:6789/0,mon2=192.168.0.42:6789/0,mon3=192.168.0.43:6789/0}
            election epoch 64, quorum 0,1,2 mon1,mon2,mon3
        mgr active: mon1 standbys: mon2, mon3
     osdmap e98: 3 osds: 3 up, 3 in
            flags sortbitwise,require_jewel_osds
      pgmap v695: 192 pgs, 2 pools, 3920 bytes data, 2 objects
            112 MB used, 26782 MB / 26894 MB avail
                 128 creating+incomplete
                  64 active+clean
```

The output of ceph health detail shows the reason why, and we see the 2147483647 error:

```
pg 2.7a is creating+incomplete, acting [0,2,1,2147483647] (reducing pool broken_ecpool min_size from 4
may help; search ceph.com/docs for 'incomplete')
pg 2.79 is creating+incomplete, acting [1,0,2,2147483647] (reducing pool broken_ecpool min_size from 4
may help; search ceph.com/docs for 'incomplete')
pg 2.78 is creating+incomplete, acting [1,0,2147483647,2] (reducing pool broken_ecpool min_size from 4
may help; search ceph.com/docs for 'incomplete')
pg 2.7f is creating+incomplete, acting [0,2,1,2147483647] (reducing pool broken_ecpool min_size from 4
may help; search ceph.com/docs for 'incomplete')
```

If you encounter this error and it is a result of your erasure profile being larger than your number of hosts or racks, depending on how you have designed your CRUSH map, then the only real solution is to either drop the number of shards or increase the number of hosts.

Summary

In this chapter you have learnt what erasure coding is and how it is implemented in Ceph. You should also have an understanding of the different configuration options possible when creating erasure-coded pools and their suitability for different types of scenarios and workloads.

5
Developing with Librados

Ceph provides block, file, and object storage via the built-in interfaces which will meet the requirements of a large number of users. However, in some scenarios where an application is developed internally, there may be benefits to directly interfacing it into Ceph via the use of librados. Librados is the Ceph library that allows applications to directly read and write objects to the RADOS layer in Ceph.

We will cover the following topics in this chapter:

- What is librados?
- How to use librados and what languages it supports
- How to write an example librados application
- How to write a librados application that stores image files in Ceph using Python
- How to write a librados application using atomic operations using C++

What is librados?

Librados is the Ceph library which you can include in your own applications to allow you to directly talk to a Ceph cluster using the native protocols. As librados communicates with Ceph using its native communication protocols, it allows your application to harness the full power, speed, and flexibility of Ceph, instead of having to make use of high-level protocols like Amazon S3. A vast array of functions allows your application to read and write simple objects all the way to advanced operations, where you might want to wrap several operations in a transaction or run them asynchronously. Librados is available for several languages, including C, C++, Python, PHP, and Java.

How to use librados?

To get started with librados, a development environment is needed. For the examples in this chapter, one of the monitor nodes can be used to act as both the development environment and the client to run the developed application. The examples in this book assume you are using a Debian based distribution:

1. Firstly, install the base build tools for the operating system:

   ```
   $ sudo apt-get install build-essential
   ```

   The preceding command gives the following output:

   ```
   vagrant@mon1:~$ sudo apt-get install build-essential
   Reading package lists... Done
   Building dependency tree
   Reading state information... Done
   The following additional packages will be installed:
     dpkg-dev g++ g++-5 libalgorithm-diff-perl libalgorithm-diff-xs-perl libalgorithm-merge-perl
     libstdc++-5-dev
   Suggested packages:
     debian-keyring g++-multilib g++-5-multilib gcc-5-doc libstdc++6-5-dbg libstdc++-5-doc
   The following NEW packages will be installed:
     build-essential dpkg-dev g++ g++-5 libalgorithm-diff-perl libalgorithm-diff-xs-perl
     libalgorithm-merge-perl libstdc++-5-dev
   0 upgraded, 8 newly installed, 0 to remove and 93 not upgraded.
   Need to get 10.4 MB of archives.
   After this operation, 41.0 MB of additional disk space will be used.
   Do you want to continue? [Y/n]
   ```

2. Install the librados development library:

   ```
   $ sudo apt-get install librados-dev
   ```

   The preceding command gives the following output:

   ```
   vagrant@mon1:~$ sudo apt-get install librados-dev
   Reading package lists... Done
   Building dependency tree
   Reading state information... Done
   The following NEW packages will be installed:
     librados-dev
   0 upgraded, 1 newly installed, 0 to remove and 93 not upgraded.
   Need to get 42.0 MB of archives.
   After this operation, 358 MB of additional disk space will be used.
   Get:1 http://download.ceph.com/debian-jewel xenial/main amd64 librados-dev amd64 10.2.5-1xenial [42.0 MB]
   Fetched 42.0 MB in 30s (1,359 kB/s)
   Selecting previously unselected package librados-dev.
   (Reading database ... 40080 files and directories currently installed.)
   Preparing to unpack .../librados-dev_10.2.5-1xenial_amd64.deb ...
   Unpacking librados-dev (10.2.5-1xenial) ...
   Processing triggers for man-db (2.7.5-1) ...
   Setting up librados-dev (10.2.5-1xenial) ...
   ```

3. Now that your environment is complete, let's create a quick application written in C to establish a connection to the test Ceph cluster:

```
$ mkdir test_app
$ cd test_app
```

4. Create a file called `test_app.c` with your favorite text editor and place the following in it:

```
#include <rados/librados.h>
#include <stdio.h>
#include <stdlib.h>

rados_t rados = NULL;

int exit_func();


int main(int argc, const char **argv)
{
  int ret = 0;
  ret = rados_create(&rados, "admin"); // Use the
  client.admin keyring
  if (ret < 0) { // Check that the rados object was created
    printf("couldn't initialize rados! error %d\n", ret);
    ret = EXIT_FAILURE;
    exit_func;
  }
  else
    printf("RADOS initialized\n");

  ret = rados_conf_read_file(rados, "/etc/ceph/ceph.conf");
  if (ret < 0) { //Parse the ceph.conf to obtain cluster details
    printf("failed to parse config options! error %d\n", ret);
    ret = EXIT_FAILURE;
    exit_func();
  }
  else
    printf("Ceph config parsed\n");

  ret = rados_connect(rados); //Initiate connection to the
  Ceph cluster
  if (ret < 0) {
    printf("couldn't connect to cluster! error %d\n", ret);
    ret = EXIT_FAILURE;
    exit_func;
  } else {
```

```
        printf("Connected to the rados cluster\n");
    }

    exit_func(); //End of example, call exit_func to clean
    up and finish


}


int exit_func ()
{
    rados_shutdown(rados); //Destroy connection to the
    Ceph cluster
    printf("RADOS connection destroyed\n");
    printf("The END\n");
    exit(0);
}
```

5. Compile the test application, by running the following command:

   $ gcc test_app.c -o test_app -lrados

 It's important to note that you need to tell gcc to link to the librados
library to make use of its functions.

6. Then, test that the app works by running it. Don't forget to run it as root or use
   sudo, otherwise you won't have access to the Ceph keyring:

   sudo ./test_app

The preceding command gives the following output:

```
vagrant@mon1:~/test_app$ sudo ./test_app
RADOS initialised
Ceph config parsed
Connected to the rados cluster
RADOS connection destroyed
The END
```

The test application simply reads your `ceph.conf` configuration, uses it to establish a connection to your Ceph cluster, and then disconnects. It's hardly the most exciting of applications but it tests that the basic infrastructure is in place and is working and establishes a foundation for the rest of the examples in this chapter.

Example librados application

We will now go through some example librados applications which use librados to get a better understanding of what you can accomplish with the library.

The following example will take you through the steps to create an application which, when given an image file as a parameter, will store the image as an object in a Ceph cluster and store various attributes about the image file as object attributes. The application will also allow you to retrieve the object and export it as an image file. This example will be written in Python, which is also supported by librados. The following example also uses the **Python Imaging Library** (PIL) to read an image's size and the **Argument Parser library** to read command-line parameters:

1. We first need to install the librados Python bindings and image manipulation libraries:

   ```
   $ sudo apt-get install python-rados python-imaging
   ```

   The preceding command gives the following output:

```
Reading package lists... Done
Building dependency tree
Reading state information... Done
python-rados is already the newest version (10.2.5-1xenial).
python-rados set to manually installed.
The following additional packages will be installed:
  libjbig0 libjpeg-turbo8 libjpeg8 liblcms2-2 libtiff5 libwebp5 libwebpmux1 python-pil
Suggested packages:
  liblcms2-utils python-pil-doc python-pil-dbg
The following NEW packages will be installed:
  libjbig0 libjpeg-turbo8 libjpeg8 liblcms2-2 libtiff5 libwebp5 libwebpmux1 python-imaging python-pil
0 upgraded, 9 newly installed, 0 to remove and 93 not upgraded.
Need to get 916 kB of archives.
After this operation, 3,303 kB of additional disk space will be used.
Do you want to continue? [Y/n] y
```

2. Create a new file for your Python application ending with the extension `.py` and enter the following into it:

   ```
   import rados, sys, argparse
   from PIL import Image
   ```

```python
#Argument Parser used to read parameters and generate --help
parser = argparse.ArgumentParser(description='Image to RADOS
Object Utility')
parser.add_argument('--action', dest='action', action='store',
required=True, help='Either upload or download image to/from
Ceph')
parser.add_argument('--image-file', dest='imagefile',
action='store', required=True, help='The image file to
upload to RADOS')
parser.add_argument('--object-name', dest='objectname',
action='store', required=True, help='The name of the
RADOS object')
parser.add_argument('--pool', dest='pool', action='store',
required=True, help='The name of the RADOS pool to store
the object')
parser.add_argument('--comment', dest='comment', action=
'store', help='A comment to store with the object')


args = parser.parse_args()

try: #Read ceph.conf config file to obtain monitors
  cluster = rados.Rados(conffile='/etc/ceph/ceph.conf')
except:
  print "Error reading Ceph configuration"
  sys.exit(1)

try: #Connect to the Ceph cluster
  cluster.connect()
except:
  print "Error connecting to Ceph Cluster"
  sys.exit(1)

try: #Open specified RADOS pool
  ioctx = cluster.open_ioctx(args.pool)
except:
  print "Error opening pool: " + args.pool
  cluster.shutdown()
  sys.exit(1)

if args.action == 'upload': #If action is to upload
  try: #Open image file in read binary mode
    image=open(args.imagefile,'rb')
    im=Image.open(args.imagefile)
  except:
    print "Error opening image file"
    ioctx.close()
    cluster.shutdown()
```

```
      sys.exit(1)
    print "Image size is x=" + str(im.size[0]) + " y=" +
    str(im.size[1])
    try: #Write the contents of image file to object and add
    attributes
      ioctx.write_full(args.objectname,image.read())
      ioctx.set_xattr(args.objectname,'xres',str(im.size[0])
      +"\n")
      ioctx.set_xattr(args.objectname,'yres',str(im.size[1])
      +"\n")
      im.close()
      if args.comment:
        ioctx.set_xattr(args.objectname,'comment',args.comment
        +"\n")
    except:
      print "Error writing object or attributes"
      ioctx.close()
      cluster.shutdown()
      sys.exit(1)
    image.close()
  elif args.action == 'download':
    try: #Open image file in write binary mode
      image=open(args.imagefile,'wb')
    except:
      print "Error opening image file"
      ioctx.close()
      cluster.shutdown()
      sys.exit(1)
    try: #Write object to image file
      image.write(ioctx.read(args.objectname))
    except:
      print "Error writing object to image file"
      ioctx.close()
      cluster.shutdown()
      sys.exit(1)
    image.close()
  else:
    print "Please specify --action as either upload or download"
  ioctx.close() #Close connection to pool
  cluster.shutdown() #Close connection to Ceph
  #The End
```

3. Test the `help` functionality generated by the Argument Parser library:

```
$ sudo python app1.py --help
```

The preceding command gives the following output:

```
vagrant@mon1:~$ sudo python app1.py --help
usage: app1.py [-h] --action ACTION --image-file IMAGEFILE --object-name
               OBJECTNAME --pool POOL [--comment COMMENT]

Image to RADOS Object Utility

optional arguments:
  -h, --help            show this help message and exit
  --action ACTION       Either upload or download image to/from Ceph
  --image-file IMAGEFILE
                        The image file to upload to RADOS
  --object-name OBJECTNAME
                        The name of the RADOS object
  --pool POOL           The name of the RADOS pool to store the object
  --comment COMMENT     A comment to store with the object
```

4. Download the Ceph logo to use as a test image:

```
wget http://docs.ceph.com/docs/master/_static/logo.png
```

The preceding command gives the following output:

```
vagrant@mon1:~$ wget http://docs.ceph.com/docs/master/_static/logo.png
--2017-02-08 20:37:01--  http://docs.ceph.com/docs/master/_static/logo.png
Resolving docs.ceph.com (docs.ceph.com)... 158.69.67.53
Connecting to docs.ceph.com (docs.ceph.com)|158.69.67.53|:80... connected.
HTTP request sent, awaiting response... 200 OK
Length: 3898 (3.8K) [image/png]
Saving to: 'logo.png'

logo.png            100%[===================================>]   3.81K  --.-KB/s    in 0s

2017-02-08 20:37:01 (106 MB/s) - 'logo.png' saved [3898/3898]
```

5. Run our Python application to read an image file and upload it to Ceph as an object:

```
$ sudo python app1.py --action=upload --image-file=test1.png
--object-name=image_test --pool=rbd --comment="Ceph Logo"
```

The preceding command gives the following output:

```
vagrant@mon1:~$ sudo python app1.py --action=upload --image-file=logo.png --object-name=image_test --pool
=rbd --comment="Ceph Logo"
Image size is x=140 y=38
```

6. Verify that the object has been created:

```
$ sudo rados -p rbd ls
```

The preceding command gives the following output:

```
vagrant@mon1:~$ sudo rados -p rbd ls
image_test
```

7. Use `rados` to verify that the attributes have been added to the object:

```
$ sudo rados -p rbd listxattr image_test
```

The preceding command gives the following output:

```
vagrant@mon1:~$ sudo rados -p rbd ls
image_test
vagrant@mon1:~$ sudo rados -p rbd listxattr image_test
comment
xres
yres
```

8. Use `rados` to verify the attributes' contents, as shown in the following screenshot:

```
vagrant@mon1:~$ sudo rados -p rbd getxattr image_test comment
Ceph Logo
vagrant@mon1:~$ sudo rados -p rbd getxattr image_test xres
140
vagrant@mon1:~$ sudo rados -p rbd getxattr image_test yres
38
```

Example of the librados application with atomic operations

In the previous librados application example, an object was created on the Ceph cluster and then the object's attributes were added. In most cases, this two stage operation may be fine, however some applications might require that the creation of the object and its attributes are atomic. That is to say, that if there was an interruption of service, the object should only exist if it has all its attributes set, otherwise the Ceph cluster should roll back the transaction. The following example, written in C++, shows how to use librados atomic operations to ensure transaction consistency across multiple operations. The example will write an object and then prompt the user if they wish to abort the transaction. If they choose to abort then the object write operation will be rolled back. If they choose to continue then the attributes will be written and the whole transaction will be committed. Perform the following steps:

1. Create a new file with a `.cc` extension and place the following into it:

```
#include <cctype>
#include <rados/librados.hpp>
#include <iostream>
#include <string>

void exit_func(int ret);

librados::Rados rados;

int main(int argc, const char **argv)
{
  int ret = 0;

  // Define variables
  const char *pool_name = "rbd";
  std::string object_string("I am an atomic object\n");
  std::string attribute_string("I am an atomic attribute\n");
  std::string object_name("atomic_object");
  librados::IoCtx io_ctx;

  // Create the Rados object and initialize it
  {
    ret = rados.init("admin"); // Use the default client.admin
    keyring
    if (ret < 0) {
      std::cerr << "Failed to initialize rados! error " << ret
      << std::endl;
      ret = EXIT_FAILURE;
```

```
    }
  }

  // Read the ceph config file in its default location
  ret = rados.conf_read_file("/etc/ceph/ceph.conf");
  if (ret < 0) {
    std::cerr << "Failed to parse config file "
              << "! Error" << ret << std::endl;
    ret = EXIT_FAILURE;
  }

  // Connect to the Ceph cluster
  ret = rados.connect();
  if (ret < 0) {
    std::cerr << "Failed to connect to cluster! Error " << ret
    << std::endl;
    ret = EXIT_FAILURE;
  } else {
    std::cout << "Connected to the Ceph cluster" << std::endl;
  }

  // Create connection to the Rados pool
  ret = rados.ioctx_create(pool_name, io_ctx);
  if (ret < 0) {
    std::cerr << "Failed to connect to pool! Error: " << ret <<
    std::endl;
    ret = EXIT_FAILURE;
  } else {
    std::cout << "Connected to pool: " << pool_name <<
    std::endl;
  }

  librados::bufferlist object_bl; // Initialize a bufferlist
  object_bl.append(object_string); // Add our object text
  string to the bufferlist
  librados::ObjectWriteOperation write_op; // Create a write
  transaction
  write_op.write_full(object_bl); // Write our bufferlist to the
  transaction
  std::cout << "Object: " << object_name << " has been written
  to transaction" << std::endl;
  char c;
  std::cout << "Would you like to abort transaction? (Y/N)? ";
  std::cin >> c;
  if (toupper( c ) == 'Y') {
    std::cout << "Transaction has been aborted, so object will
    not actually be written" << std::endl;
    exit_func(99);
```

```
  }
  librados::bufferlist attr_bl; // Initialize another bufferlist
  attr_bl.append(attribute_string); // Add our attribute to the
  bufferlist
  write_op.setxattr("atomic_attribute", attr_bl); // Write our
  attribute to our transaction
  std::cout << "Attribute has been written to transaction" <<
  std::endl;
  ret = io_ctx.operate(object_name, &write_op); // Commit the
  transaction
  if (ret < 0) {
    std::cerr << "failed to do compound write! error " << ret <<
    std::endl;
    ret = EXIT_FAILURE;
  } else {
    std::cout << "We wrote the transaction containing our object
    and attribute" << object_name << std::endl;
  }

}

void exit_func(int ret)
{
  // Clean up and exit
  rados.shutdown();
  exit(ret);
}
```

2. Compile the source using g++:

```
g++ atomic.cc -o atomic -lrados -std=c++11
```

3. We can now run the application. First, let's run through it and abort the transaction:

```
vagrant@mon1:~$ sudo ./atomic
Connected to the rados cluster
Connected to pool: rbd
Object: atomic_object has been written to transaction
Would you like to abort transaction? (Y/N)? y
Transaction has been aborted, so object will not actually be written
vagrant@mon1:~$ sudo rados -p rbd ls
```

The preceding screenshot shows that, even though we sent a write object command, as the transaction was not committed, the object was never actually written to the Ceph cluster.

4. Now let's run the application again and, this time, let it continue the transaction:

```
vagrant@mon1:~$ sudo ./atomic
Connected to the rados cluster
Connected to pool: rbd
Object: atomic_object has been written to transaction
Would you like to abort transaction? (Y/N)? n
Attribute has been written to transaction
We wrote the transaction containing our object and attributeatomic_object
vagrant@mon1:~$ sudo rados -p rbd ls
atomic_object
vagrant@mon1:~$ sudo rados -p rbd getxattr atomic_object atomic_attribute
I am an atomic attribute
```

As you can see, this time the object was written along with its attribute.

Example of the librados application that uses watchers and notifiers

The following librados application is written in C and shows how to use the `watch` or `notify` functionality in RADOS. Ceph enables a client to create a watcher on an object and receive notifications from a completely separate client connected to the same cluster.

The watcher functionality is implemented via callback functions. When you call the librados function to create the watcher, two of the arguments are for callback functions, one is for what to do when a notification is received and another is for what to do if the watcher loses contact or encounters an error with the object. These callback functions then contain the code you want to run when a notification or error occurs.

This simple form of messaging is commonly used to instruct a client that has a RBD in use that a snapshot is wished to be taken. The client who wishes to take a snapshot sends a notification to all clients that may be watching the RBD object so that it can flush its cache and possibly make sure the filesystem is in a consistent state.

The following example creates a watcher on an object named `my_object` and then waits. When it receives a notification, it will display the payload and then send a received message back to the notifier.

1. Create a new file with a `.c` extension and place the following into it:

```c
#include <stdio.h>
#include <stdlib.h>
#include <string.h>
#include <syslog.h>

#include <rados/librados.h>
#include <rados/rados_types.h>

uint64_t cookie;
rados_ioctx_t io;
rados_t cluster;
char cluster_name[] = "ceph";
char user_name[] = "client.admin";
char object[] = "my_object";
char pool[] = "rbd";

/* Watcher callback function - called when watcher receives a
notification */
void watch_notify2_cb(void *arg, uint64_t notify_id, uint64_t
cookie, uint64_t notifier_gid, void *data, size_t data_len)
{
  const char *notify_oid = 0;
  char *temp = (char*)data+4;
  int ret;
  printf("Message from Notifier: %s\n",temp);
  rados_notify_ack(io, object, notify_id, cookie, "Received", 8);
}

/* Watcher error callback function - called if watcher encounters
an error */
void watch_notify2_errcb(void *arg, uint64_t cookie, int err)
{
  printf("Removing Watcher on object %s\n",object);
  err = rados_unwatch2(io,cookie);
  printf("Creating Watcher on object %s\n",object);
  err = rados_watch2(io,object,&cookie,watch_notify2_cb,
  watch_notify2_errcb,NULL);
  if (err < 0) {
    fprintf(stderr, "Cannot create watcher on %s/%s: %s\n", object,
    pool, strerror(-err));
    rados_ioctx_destroy(io);
```

```
    rados_shutdown(cluster);
    exit(1);
  }
}

int main (int argc, char **argv)
{
  int err;
  uint64_t flags;

  /* Create Rados object */
  err = rados_create2(&cluster, cluster_name, user_name, flags);
  if (err < 0) {
    fprintf(stderr, "Couldn't create the cluster object!: %s\n",
    strerror(-err));
    exit(EXIT_FAILURE);
  } else {
    printf("Created the rados object.\n");
  }


  /* Read a Ceph configuration file to configure the cluster
  handle. */
  err = rados_conf_read_file(cluster, "/etc/ceph/ceph.conf");
  if (err < 0) {
    fprintf(stderr, "Cannot read config file: %s\n",
    strerror(-err));
    exit(EXIT_FAILURE);
  } else {
    printf("Read the config file.\n");
  }
  /* Connect to the cluster */
  err = rados_connect(cluster);
  if (err < 0) {
    fprintf(stderr, "Cannot connect to cluster: %s\n",
    strerror(-err));
    exit(EXIT_FAILURE);
  } else {
    printf("\n Connected to the cluster.\n");
  }

  /* Create connection to the Rados pool */
  err = rados_ioctx_create(cluster, pool, &io);
  if (err < 0) {
    fprintf(stderr, "Cannot open rados pool %s: %s\n", pool,
    strerror(-err));
    rados_shutdown(cluster);
    exit(1);
```

```
    }

    /* Create the Rados Watcher */
    printf("Creating Watcher on object %s/%s\n",pool,object);
    err = rados_watch2(io,object,&cookie,watch_notify2_cb,
    watch_notify2_errcb,NULL);
    if (err < 0) {
      fprintf(stderr, "Cannot create watcher on object %s/%s: %s\n",
      pool, object, strerror(-err));
      rados_ioctx_destroy(io);
      rados_shutdown(cluster);
      exit(1);
    }

    /* Loop whilst waiting for notifier */
    while(1){
      sleep(1);
    }
    /* Clean up */
    rados_ioctx_destroy(io);
    rados_shutdown(cluster);
  }
```

2. Compile the `watcher` example code:

    ```
    $ gcc watcher.c -o watcher -lrados
    ```

3. Run the `watcher` example application:

```
vagrant@mon1:~$ sudo ./watcher
Created the rados object.
Read the config file.

Connected to the cluster.
Creating Watcher on object rbd/my_object
```

4. The watcher is now waiting for a notification. In another Terminal window, using `rados`, send a notification to the `my_object` object which is being watched:

```
vagrant@mon1:~$ sudo rados -p rbd notify my_object "Hello There!"
reply client.24135 cookie 29079312 : 8 bytes
00000000  52 65 63 69 65 76 65 64                           |Recieved|
00000008
```

5. You can see that the notification was sent and an acknowledgement notification has been received back. If we look at the first Terminal window again, we can see the message from the notifier:

```
vagrant@mon1:~$ sudo ./watcher
Created the rados object.
Read the config file.

Connected to the cluster.
Creating Watcher on object rbd/my_object
Message from Notifier: Hello There!
```

Summary

This concludes the chapter on developing applications with librados. You should now feel comfortable with the basic concepts of how to include librados functionality in your application and how to read and write objects to your Ceph cluster. It would be recommended to read the official librados documentation in more detail if you intend to develop an application with librados, so that you can gain a better understanding of the full range of functions that are available.

6
Distributed Computation with Ceph RADOS Classes

An often overlooked feature of Ceph is the ability to load custom code directly into OSD, which can then be executed from within a librados application. This allows you to take advantage of the large distributed scale of Ceph to not only provide high-performance scale-out storage but also distribute computational tasks over OSDs to achieve mass parallel computing. This ability is realized by dynamically loading in RADOS classes to each OSD.

In this chapter you will learn the following topics:

- Example applications and benefits of using RADOS classes
- Writing a simple RADOS class in Lua
- Writing a RADOS class that simulates distributed computing

Example applications and the benefits of using RADOS classes

As mentioned earlier, with RADOS classes, code is executed directly inside the OSD code base and so can harness the combined power of all of the OSD nodes. With a typical client application approach, where the client would have to read the object from the Ceph cluster, run computations on it, and then write it back, there is a large amount of round trip overheads. Using RADOS classes dramatically reduces the amount of round trips to and from OSDs, and also the available compute power is much higher than that single client could provide. Offloading operations directly to the OSDs therefore enables a single client to dramatically increase its processing rate.

A simple example of where RADOS classes could be used is where you need to calculate a hash of every object in a RADOS pool and store each objects hash as an attribute. Having a client perform this would highlight the bottlenecks and extra latency introduced by having the client perform these operations remotely from the cluster. With a RADOS class that contains the required code to read the object calculate the hash and store it as an attribute, all that the client would need to do is send the command to OSD to execute the RADOS class.

Writing a simple RADOS class in Lua

One of the default RADOS classes in Ceph from the Kraken release onward is one that can run Lua scripts. The Lua script is dynamically passed to the Lua RADOS object class, which then executes the contents of the script. The scripts are typically passed in a JSON-formatted string to the object class. Although this brings advantages over the traditional RADOS object classes, which need to be compiled before they can be used, it also limits the complexity of what the Lua scripts can accomplish and as such thought should be given as to what method is appropriate for the task you wish to accomplish.

The following Python code example demonstrates how to create and pass a Lua script to be executed on an OSD. The Lua scripts reads the contents of the specified object and returns the string of text back in upper case, all processing is done on the remote OSD, which holds the object; the original object contents are never sent to the client.

Place the following into a file named `rados_lua.py`:

```python
import rados, json, sys

try: #Read ceph.conf config file to obtain monitors
  cluster = rados.Rados(conffile='/etc/ceph/ceph.conf')
except:
  print "Error reading Ceph configuration"
  exit(1)

try: #Connect to the Ceph cluster
  cluster.connect()
except:
  print "Error connecting to Ceph Cluster"
  exit(1)

try: #Open specified RADOS pool
  ioctx = cluster.open_ioctx("rbd")
except:
  print "Error opening pool"
```

```
    cluster.shutdown()
    exit(1)

cmd = {
    "script": """
        function upper(input, output)
            size = objclass.stat()
            data = objclass.read(0, size)
            upper_str = string.upper(data:str())
            output:append(upper_str)
        end
        objclass.register(upper)
    """,
    "handler": "upper",
}

ret, data = ioctx.execute(str(sys.argv[1]), 'lua', 'eval_json',
json.dumps(cmd))
print data[:ret]

ioctx.close() #Close connection to pool
cluster.shutdown() #Close connection to Ceph
```

Let's now create a test object with all lowercase characters:

```
echo this string was in lowercase | sudo rados -p rbd put LowerObject -
```

The Lua object class by default is not allowed to be called by OSDs; we need to add the following to all the OSDs in their `ceph.conf`:

```
[osd]
osd class load list = *
osd class default list = *
```

And now run our Python librados application:

```
sudo python rados_lua.py LowerObject
```

The preceding command gives the following output:

```
vagrant@mon1:~$ sudo python rados_lua.py LowerObject
THIS STRING WAS IN LOWERCASE
```

You should see that the text from our object has been converted all into uppercase. You can see from the Python code earlier that we are not doing any of the conversion in the local Python code and it's all being done remotely on OSD.

Writing a RADOS class that simulates distributed computing

As mentioned in the example given earlier, although using the Lua object class reduces the complexity to use RADOS object classes, there is a limit to what you can currently achieve. In order to write a class that is capable of performing more advanced processing, we need to fall back to writing the class in C. We will then need to compile the new class into the Ceph source.

To demonstrate this, we will write a new RADOS object class that will calculate the MD5 hash of the specified object and then store it as an attribute of the object. This process will be repeated 1000 times to simulate a busy environment and also to make the runtime easier to measure. We will then compare the operating speed of doing this via the object class versus calculating the MD5 hash on the client. Although this is still a fairly basic task, it will allow us to produce a controlled repeatable scenario and will allow us to compare the speed of completing a task client side versus doing it directly on the OSD via a RADOS class. It will also serve as a good foundation to enable understanding on how to build more advanced applications.

Preparing the build environment

Use the following command to clone the Ceph git repository:

```
git clone https://github.com/ceph/ceph.git
```

The preceding command will give the following output:

```
vagrant@ansible:~$ git clone https://github.com/ceph/ceph.git
Cloning into 'ceph'...
remote: Counting objects: 500133, done.
remote: Compressing objects: 100% (21/21), done.
remote: Total 500133 (delta 12), reused 2 (delta 2), pack-reused 500110
Receiving objects: 100% (500133/500133), 203.37 MiB | 2.38 MiB/s, done.
Resolving deltas: 100% (394234/394234), done.
Checking connectivity... done.
```

Once we have cloned the Ceph git repository, we need to edit the CMakeLists.txt file and add in a section for our new class that we are going to write.

Edit the following file in the source tree:

~/ceph/src/cls/CMakeLists.txt

Also, place the following in the file:

```
# cls_md5
set(cls_md5_srcs md5/cls_md5.cc)
add_library(cls_md5 SHARED ${cls_md5_srcs})
set_target_properties(cls_md5 PROPERTIES
  VERSION "1.0.0"
  SOVERSION "1"
  INSTALL_RPATH "")
install(TARGETS cls_md5 DESTINATION ${cls_dir})
target_link_libraries(cls_md5 crypto)
list(APPEND cls_embedded_srcs ${cls_md5_srcs})
```

Once the `cmakelist.txt` file is updated, we can get `cmake` to make the build environment by running the following command:

do_cmake.sh

The preceding command will give the following output:

```
-- Configuring done
-- Generating done
-- Build files have been written to: /home/vagrant/ceph/build
+ cat
+ echo 40000
+ echo done.
done.
```

This will create a `build` directory in the source tree.

In order for us to build the RADOS class, we need to install the required packages that contains the `make` command:

sudo apt-get install build-essentials

There is also a `install-deps.sh` file in the Ceph source tree, which will install the remaining required packages when run.

RADOS class

The following code sample is a RADOS class which when executed reads the object, calculates the MD5 hash, and then writes it as an attribute to the object without any client involvement. Each time this class is called, it repeats this operation a 1000 times locally to OSD and only notifies the client at the end of this processing. We have the following steps to perform:

1. Create the directory for our new RADOS class:

   ```
   mkdir ~/ceph/src/cls/md5
   ```

2. Now create the C++ source file:

   ```
   ~/ceph/src/cls/md5/cls_md5.cc
   ```

3. Place the following code into it:

   ```
   #include "objclass/objclass.h"
   #include <openssl/md5.h>

   CLS_VER(1,0)
   CLS_NAME(md5)

   cls_handle_t h_class;
   cls_method_handle_t h_calc_md5;

   static int calc_md5(cls_method_context_t hctx, bufferlist *in,
   bufferlist *out)
   {
     char md5string[33];

     for(int i = 0; i < 1000; ++i)
     {
       size_t size;
       int ret = cls_cxx_stat(hctx, &size, NULL);
       if (ret < 0)
         return ret;

       bufferlist data;
       ret = cls_cxx_read(hctx, 0, size, &data);
       if (ret < 0)
         return ret;
       unsigned char md5out[16];
       MD5((unsigned char*)data.c_str(), data.length(), md5out);
       for(int i = 0; i < 16; ++i)
         sprintf(&md5string[i*2], "%02x", (unsigned int)md5out[i]);
   ```

```
    CLS_LOG(0,"Loop:%d - %s",i,md5string);
    bufferlist attrbl;
    attrbl.append(md5string);
    ret = cls_cxx_setxattr(hctx, "MD5", &attrbl);
    if (ret < 0)
    {
      CLS_LOG(0, "Error setting attribute");
      return ret;
    }
  }
  out->append((const char*)md5string, sizeof(md5string));
  return 0;
}

void __cls_init()
{
  CLS_LOG(0, "loading cls_md5");
  cls_register("md5", &h_class);
  cls_register_cxx_method(h_class, "calc_md5", CLS_METHOD_RD |
  CLS_METHOD_WR, calc_md5, &h_calc_md5)
}
```

4. Change into the `build` directory created previously and create our new RADOS class using `make`:

```
cd ~/ceph/build
make cls_md5
```

The preceding commands will give the following output:

```
vagrant@ansible:~/ceph/build$ make cls_md5
Scanning dependencies of target cls_md5
[  0%] Building CXX object src/cls/CMakeFiles/cls_md5.dir/md5/cls_md5.cc.o
[100%] Linking CXX shared library ../../lib/libcls_md5.so
[100%] Built target cls_md5
```

5. We now need to copy our new class to OSDs in our cluster:

```
sudo scp vagrant@ansible:/home/vagrant/ceph/build/lib/libcls_md5.so*
/usr/lib/rados-classes/
```

The preceding command will give the following output:

```
vagrant@osd2:~$ sudo scp vagrant@ansible:/home/vagrant/ceph/build/lib/libcls_md5.so* /usr/lib/rados-classes/
vagrant@ansible's password:
libcls_md5.so                                        100%  155KB 155.0KB/s   00:00
libcls_md5.so.1                                      100%  155KB 155.0KB/s   00:00
libcls_md5.so.1.0.0                                  100%  155KB 155.0KB/s   00:00
```

Also, restart the OSD for it to load the class.

You will now see in the Ceph OSD log that it is loading our new class:

```
2017-05-10 19:47:57.251739 7fdb99ca2700  1 leveldb: Compacting 4@0 + 4@1 files
2017-05-10 19:47:57.260570 7fdba409fa40  1 journal _open /var/lib/ceph/osd/ceph-1/journal fd 28: 1073741824 bytes, bl
ock size 4096 bytes, directio = 1, aio = 1
2017-05-10 19:47:57.280605 7fdba409fa40  1 journal _open /var/lib/ceph/osd/ceph-1/journal fd 28: 1073741824 bytes, bl
ock size 4096 bytes, directio = 1, aio = 1
2017-05-10 19:47:57.283291 7fdba409fa40  1 filestore(/var/lib/ceph/osd/ceph-1) upgrade
2017-05-10 19:47:57.300701 7fdba409fa40  0 <cls> /home/vagrant/ceph/src/cls/md5/cls_md5.cc:46: loading cls_md5
2017-05-10 19:47:57.301246 7fdba409fa40  0 <cls> /tmp/buildd/ceph-11.2.0/src/cls/cephfs/cls_cephfs.cc:198: loading ce
phfs
2017-05-10 19:47:57.308766 7fdba409fa40  0 <cls> /tmp/buildd/ceph-11.2.0/src/cls/hello/cls_hello.cc:296: loading cls_
hello
2017-05-10 19:47:57.318132 7fdba409fa40  0 osd.1 279 crush map has features 2200130813952, adjusting msqr requires fo
r clients
2017-05-10 19:47:57.318940 7fdba409fa40  0 osd.1 279 crush map has features 2200130813952 was 8705, adjusting msqr re
quires for mons
2017-05-10 19:47:57.318966 7fdba409fa40  0 osd.1 279 crush map has features 2200130813952, adjusting msqr requires fo
r osds
```

This needs to be repeated for all OSD nodes in the cluster.

Client librados applications

As mentioned earlier, we will use two librados applications, one to calculate the MD5 hash directly on the client and another to call our RADOS class and have it calculate the MD5 hash. The two applications both need to be run from the monitor nodes in the test cluster, but can be compiled on any node and copied across if desired. For the purpose of this example, we will compile the applications directly on the monitor nodes.

Before we start, let's make sure that the build environment is present on the monitor node:

```
apt-get install build-essential librados-dev
```

Calculating MD5 on the client

The following code sample is the librados client-side application, which will read the object from the OSD, calculate the MD5 hash of the object on the client, and write it back as an attribute to the object. This is doing the calculation and storage in the same way as the RADOS class, with the only difference being the location of the processing.

Create a new file named rados_md5.cc and place the following into it:

```
#include <cctype>
#include <rados/librados.hpp>
#include <iostream>
#include <string>
#include <openssl/md5.h>
```

```
void exit_func(int ret);

librados::Rados rados;

int main(int argc, const char **argv)
{
  int ret = 0;

  // Define variables
  const char *pool_name = "rbd";
  std::string object_name("LowerObject");
  librados::IoCtx io_ctx;

  // Create the Rados object and initialize it
  {
    ret = rados.init("admin"); // Use the default client.admin keyring
    if (ret < 0) {
      std::cerr << "Failed to initialize rados! error " << ret <<
      std::endl;
      ret = EXIT_FAILURE;
    }
  }

  // Read the ceph config file in its default location
  ret = rados.conf_read_file("/etc/ceph/ceph.conf");
  if (ret < 0) {
    std::cerr << "Failed to parse config file "
              << "! Error" << ret << std::endl;
    ret = EXIT_FAILURE;
  }

  // Connect to the Ceph cluster
  ret = rados.connect();
  if (ret < 0) {
    std::cerr << "Failed to connect to cluster! Error " << ret <<
    std::endl;
    ret = EXIT_FAILURE;
  } else {
    std::cout << "Connected to the Ceph cluster" << std::endl;
  }

  // Create connection to the Rados pool
  ret = rados.ioctx_create(pool_name, io_ctx);
  if (ret < 0) {
    std::cerr << "Failed to connect to pool! Error: " << ret <<
    std::endl;
    ret = EXIT_FAILURE;
  } else {
```

```
      std::cout << "Connected to pool: " << pool_name << std::endl;
  }
  for(int i = 0; i < 1000; ++i)
  {
    size_t size;
    int ret = io_ctx.stat(object_name, &size, NULL);
    if (ret < 0)
      return ret;

    librados::bufferlist data;
    ret = io_ctx.read(object_name, data, size, 0);
    if (ret < 0)
      return ret;
    unsigned char md5out[16];
    MD5((unsigned char*)data.c_str(), data.length(), md5out);
    char md5string[33];
    for(int i = 0; i < 16; ++i)
      sprintf(&md5string[i*2], "%02x", (unsigned int)md5out[i]);
    librados::bufferlist attrbl;
    attrbl.append(md5string);
    ret = io_ctx.setxattr(object_name, "MD5", attrbl);
    if (ret < 0)
    {
      exit_func(1);
    }
  }
  exit_func(0);
}

void exit_func(int ret)
{
  // Clean up and exit
  rados.shutdown();
  exit(ret);
}
```

Calculating MD5 on the OSD via RADOS class

Finally, the last code sample is the librados application, which instructs OSD to calculate the MD5 hash locally without transferring any data to or from the client. You will note that the code given later has no librados read or write statements and relies purely on the `exec` function to trigger the MD5 hash creation.

Create a new file named `rados_class_md5.cc` and place the following into it:

```
#include <cctype>
#include <rados/librados.hpp>
#include <iostream>
#include <string>

void exit_func(int ret);

librados::Rados rados;

int main(int argc, const char **argv)
{
  int ret = 0;

  // Define variables
  const char *pool_name = "rbd";
  std::string object_name("LowerObject");
  librados::IoCtx io_ctx;
  // Create the Rados object and initialize it
  {
    ret = rados.init("admin"); // Use the default client.admin keyring
    if (ret < 0) {
      std::cerr << "Failed to initialize rados! error " << ret <<
      std::endl;
      ret = EXIT_FAILURE;
    }
  }

  // Read the ceph config file in its default location
  ret = rados.conf_read_file("/etc/ceph/ceph.conf");
  if (ret < 0) {
    std::cerr << "Failed to parse config file "
              << "! Error" << ret << std::endl;
    ret = EXIT_FAILURE;
  }

  // Connect to the Ceph cluster
  ret = rados.connect();
  if (ret < 0) {
    std::cerr << "Failed to connect to cluster! Error " << ret <<
    std::endl;
    ret = EXIT_FAILURE;
  } else {
    std::cout << "Connected to the Ceph cluster" << std::endl;
  }

  // Create connection to the Rados pool
```

```
      ret = rados.ioctx_create(pool_name, io_ctx);
      if (ret < 0) {
        std::cerr << "Failed to connect to pool! Error: " << ret <<
        std::endl;
        ret = EXIT_FAILURE;
      } else {
        std::cout << "Connected to pool: " << pool_name <<
        std::endl;
      }
      librados::bufferlist in, out;
      io_ctx.exec(object_name, "md5", "calc_md5", in, out);
      exit_func(0);

    }
    void exit_func(int ret)
    {
      // Clean up and exit
      rados.shutdown();
      exit(ret);
    }
```

We can now compile both applications:

```
vagrant@mon1:~$ g++ rados_class_md5.cc -o rados_class_md5 -lrados -std=c++11
vagrant@mon1:~$ g++ rados_md5.cc -o rados_md5 -lrados -lcrypto -std=c++11
```

If the applications compile successfully, there will be no output.

Testing

We will run the two librados applications using the standard Linux `time` utility to measure how long each run takes:

```
time sudo ./rados_md5
```

The preceding command will give the following output:

```
vagrant@mon1:~$ time sudo ./rados_md5
Connected to the Ceph cluster
Connected to pool: rbd

real    0m4.708s
user    0m0.084s
sys     0m1.008s
```

Let's make sure that the attribute was actually created:

```
sudo rados -p rbd getxattr LowerObject MD5
```

The preceding command will give the following output:

```
vagrant@mon1:~$ sudo rados -p rbd getxattr LowerObject MD5
9d40bae4ff2032c9eff59806298a95bdvagrant@mon1:~$
```

Let's delete the object attribute, so we can be certain that the RADOS class correctly creates it when it runs:

```
sudo rados -p rbd rmxattr LowerObject MD5
```

And now run the application that performs the MD5 calculation via the RADOS class:

```
time sudo ./rados_class_md5
```

The preceding command will give the following output:

```
vagrant@mon1:~$ time sudo ./rados_class_md5
Connected to the Ceph cluster
Connected to pool: rbd

real    0m0.038s
user    0m0.004s
sys     0m0.012s
```

As you can see, using the RADOS class method is a lot faster, in fact almost two orders of magnitude faster.

However, let's also confirm that the attribute was created and that the code ran a thousand times:

```
sudo rados -p rbd getxattr LowerObject MD5
```

The preceding command will give the following output:

```
vagrant@mon1:~$ sudo rados -p rbd getxattr LowerObject MD5
9d40bae4ff2032c9eff59806298a95bdvagrant@mon1:~$
```

Due to the logging we inserted in the RADOS class, we can also check OSD logs to confirm that the RADOS class did run a thousand times:

```
0 <cls> /home/vagrant/ceph/src/cls/md5/cls_md5.cc:30: Loop:984 - 9d40bae4ff2032c9eff59806298a95bd
0 <cls> /home/vagrant/ceph/src/cls/md5/cls_md5.cc:30: Loop:985 - 9d40bae4ff2032c9eff59806298a95bd
0 <cls> /home/vagrant/ceph/src/cls/md5/cls_md5.cc:30: Loop:986 - 9d40bae4ff2032c9eff59806298a95bd
0 <cls> /home/vagrant/ceph/src/cls/md5/cls_md5.cc:30: Loop:987 - 9d40bae4ff2032c9eff59806298a95bd
0 <cls> /home/vagrant/ceph/src/cls/md5/cls_md5.cc:30: Loop:988 - 9d40bae4ff2032c9eff59806298a95bd
0 <cls> /home/vagrant/ceph/src/cls/md5/cls_md5.cc:30: Loop:989 - 9d40bae4ff2032c9eff59806298a95bd
0 <cls> /home/vagrant/ceph/src/cls/md5/cls_md5.cc:30: Loop:990 - 9d40bae4ff2032c9eff59806298a95bd
0 <cls> /home/vagrant/ceph/src/cls/md5/cls_md5.cc:30: Loop:991 - 9d40bae4ff2032c9eff59806298a95bd
0 <cls> /home/vagrant/ceph/src/cls/md5/cls_md5.cc:30: Loop:992 - 9d40bae4ff2032c9eff59806298a95bd
0 <cls> /home/vagrant/ceph/src/cls/md5/cls_md5.cc:30: Loop:993 - 9d40bae4ff2032c9eff59806298a95bd
0 <cls> /home/vagrant/ceph/src/cls/md5/cls_md5.cc:30: Loop:994 - 9d40bae4ff2032c9eff59806298a95bd
0 <cls> /home/vagrant/ceph/src/cls/md5/cls_md5.cc:30: Loop:995 - 9d40bae4ff2032c9eff59806298a95bd
0 <cls> /home/vagrant/ceph/src/cls/md5/cls_md5.cc:30: Loop:996 - 9d40bae4ff2032c9eff59806298a95bd
0 <cls> /home/vagrant/ceph/src/cls/md5/cls_md5.cc:30: Loop:997 - 9d40bae4ff2032c9eff59806298a95bd
0 <cls> /home/vagrant/ceph/src/cls/md5/cls_md5.cc:30: Loop:998 - 9d40bae4ff2032c9eff59806298a95bd
0 <cls> /home/vagrant/ceph/src/cls/md5/cls_md5.cc:30: Loop:999 - 9d40bae4ff2032c9eff59806298a95bd
```

When repeating small tasks, the overhead of communication between the client and OSDs really adds up. By moving processing directly to OSD, we can eliminate this.

RADOS class caveats

Although we have seen the power that can be harnessed using Ceph's RADOS classes, it's important to note that this is achieved by calling your own customized code from deep inside OSDs. As a consequence, great care needs to be taken that your RADOS class is bug free. A RADOS class has the ability to modify any data on your Ceph cluster, and so accidental data corruption is easily possible. It is also possible for the RADOS class to crash the OSD process. If the class is used in large-scale cluster operations, this has the ability to affect all OSDs in the cluster and so great care should be taken to ensure that error handling is properly done to avoid errors.

Summary

You should now have an understanding on what RADOS classes are and how they can be used to speed up processing by moving tasks directly to OSD. From building simple classes via Lua to developing classes in the Ceph source tree via C++, you should now have the knowledge to build a RADOS class for whatever problem you are trying to solve. By building on this concept, there is nothing stopping you from building a larger application that can take advantage of the scale-out nature of a Ceph cluster to provide large amounts of storage and compute resource.

For more examples of how to use RADOS object classes, please consult the hello object class in the Ceph source tree found at `https://github.com/ceph/ceph/blob/master/src/cls/hello/cls_hello.cc`.

7
Monitoring Ceph

When you are operating a Ceph cluster, it's important to monitor its health and performance. By monitoring Ceph, you can be sure that your cluster is running in full health and also be able to quickly react to any issues that may arise. By capturing and graphing performance counters, you will also have the data required to tune Ceph and observe your tuning impact on your cluster.

In this chapter you will learn the following topics:

- Why it is important to monitor Ceph
- How to monitor Ceph's health
- What should be monitored
- The states of PGs and what they mean
- How to capture and Ceph's performance counters with collectd
- Example graphs using Graphite

Why it is important to monitor Ceph

The most important reason to monitor Ceph is to ensure that the cluster is running in a healthy state. If Ceph is not running in a healthy state, be it because of a failed disk or some other reason, the chances of a loss of service or data loss increase. Although Ceph is highly automated in recovering from a variety of scenarios, being aware of what is going on and when manual intervention is required is essential.

Monitoring isn't just about detecting failures, monitoring other metrics like used disk space is just as essential as knowing when a disk has failed. If your Ceph cluster fills up, it will stop accepting I/O requests and will not be able to recover from future OSD failures.

Finally, monitoring both the operating systems and Ceph's performance metrics can help you spot performance issues or identify tuning opportunities.

What should be monitored

The simple answer is everything, or as much as you can. You can never predict what scenario may be forced upon you and your cluster and having the correct monitoring and alerting in place can mean the difference between handing a situation gracefully or having a full-scale outage. A list of things that should be monitored in decreasing order of importance is as follows.

Ceph health

The most important thing to capture is the health status of Ceph. The main reporting item is the overall health status of the cluster, either Health_OK, Health_Warning, or Health_Critical. By monitoring this state, you will get alerted anytime Ceph itself thinks that something is not right. In addition to this, you may also want to capture the status of the PGs and number of degraded objects, they can provide additional information as to what might be wrong without having to actually log on to a Ceph server and use the Ceph toolset to check the status.

Operating system and hardware

It's also highly recommended that you capture the current status of the operating system running the Ceph software and also the status of the underlying hardware. Capturing things such as CPU and RAM usage will alert you to possible resource starvation before it potentially becomes critical. Also, long-term trending on this data can help to plan hardware choices for Ceph. Monitoring of the hardware to capture hardware failures, such as disks, PSUs, and fans, is also highly recommended. Most server hardware is redundant and may not be obvious unless monitored that it is running in a degraded state. In addition, monitoring network connections so that you can be sure that both NICs are available in bonded configuration are working is also a good idea.

Smart stats

Using your operating system's smart monitoring tool suite to probe the health of the disks is also a good idea. They may help to highlight failing disks or ones with abnormal error rates. For SSDs, you can also measure the wear rate of the flash cells, which is a good indication of when the SSD is likely to fail. Finally, being able to capture the temperature of the disks will allow you to make sure that your servers are not overheating.

Network

As Ceph relies on the network it runs over to be reliable, it can be beneficial to monitor network devices for errors and performance issues. Most network devices can be polled via SNMP to obtain this data. In addition, if using **jumbo frames**, you may what to consider if it is possible to create some automated ping monitoring to continuously check that jumbo frames are working correctly on your network. You never know when an unexpected change may affect the ability of your network to pass jumbo frames, causing confusion as your Ceph cluster suddenly starts going haywire.

Performance counters

By monitoring performance counters from both the operating system and Ceph, you are arming yourself with a wealth of knowledge to gain a better understanding of how your Ceph cluster is performing. If storage permits, its worth trying to capture as much of these metrics as possible; you never know when the metrics will come in handy. It's quite often the case when diagnosing a problem that a metric that was previously thought to have no connection to the issue suddenly sheds light on the actual cause. The traditional approach of only monitoring key metrics is very limiting in this regard.

Most monitoring agents that run on Linux will allow you to capture a large array of metrics from resource consumption to filesystem usage. It's worth spending time analyzing what metric you can collect and configuring them appropriately. Some of these monitoring agents will also have plugins for Ceph, which can pull out all of the performance counters from Ceph's various components, such as `osd` and `mon` nodes.

PG states – the good, the bad, and the ugly

Each placement group in Ceph has one or more statuses assigned to it; normally you want to see all your PGs with `active+clean` against them. Understanding what each state means can help us identify what is happening to PG and whether you need to take action.

The good

The following states are indication of a healthy operating cluster, no action needs to be taken.

The active state

The `active` state means that PG is in full health, and it is capable of accepting client requests.

The clean state

The `clean` state means that PG's objects are replicated the correct number of times and are all in a consistent state.

Scrubbing and deep scrubbing

Scrubbing means that Ceph checks the consistency of your data and is a normal background process. Scrubbing on its own is where Ceph checks that the objects and relevant metadata exists. When Ceph peforms a deep scrub, it compares the contents of the objects and their replicas for consistency.

The bad

The following states indicate that Ceph is not in full health, but shouldn't cause any immediate problems.

The inconsistent state

The `inconsistent` state means that during the scrub process, Ceph has found one or more objects that are inconsistent with its replicas. See the troubleshooting section later in this book on how to deal with these errors.

The backfilling, backfill_wait, recovering, recovery_wait states

These states mean that Ceph is copying or migrating data from one OSD to another. This may possibly mean that this PG has less than the desired number of copies. If it's in the wait state, it means that due to throttles on each OSD, Ceph is limiting the number of concurrent operations to reduce impact on client operations.

The degraded state

The `degraded` state means that PG is missing or has out-of-date copies of one or more objects. These will normally be corrected by the recovery/backfill process.

Remapped

In order to become active, PG is currently mapped to a different OSD or set of OSDs. This is likely to occur when OSD is down but has not been recovered to the remaining OSDs.

The ugly

These states are not ones you want to see. If you see any of the states later, it's quite likely that client access to the cluster will be affected, and unless the situation can be fixed, data loss may occur.

The incomplete state

An `incomplete` state means that Ceph is unable to find any valid copies of objects within PG across any of OSDs that are currently up in the cluster. This can either be that the objects are simply not there or the available objects are missing newer writes that may have occurred on now unavailable OSDs.

The down state

Similar to `incomplete`, the PG is missing objects that are known to possibly be on unavailable OSDs.

The backfill_toofull state

Ceph has tried to recover your data, but your OSD disks are too full and it cannot continue. Extra OSDs are needed to fix this situation.

Monitoring Ceph with collectd

Previously in this chapter, we have covered what monitoring should be done around your entire Ceph infrastructure. Although the alert monitoring is out of scope of this book, we will now look at capturing the Ceph performance metrics with collectd, storing them in Graphite and then finally creating a dashboard with graphs using Grafana. These captured metrics can then be used in the following chapter to help tune your Ceph cluster.

We will build this monitoring infrastructure on one of our monitor nodes in our test cluster. In a production cluster, it is highly recommended that it gets its own dedicated server.

Graphite

Graphite is a time series database which excels in storing large amounts of metrics and has a mature query language, which can be used by applications to manipulate the data.

We first need to install the required graphite packages:

```
sudo apt-get install graphite-api graphite-carbon graphite-web
```

The preceding command gives the following output:

```
vagrant@ansible:~$ sudo apt-get install graphite-api graphite-carbon graphite-web
Reading package lists... Done
Building dependency tree
Reading state information... Done
The following additional packages will be installed:
  fontconfig-config fonts-dejavu-core javascript-common libcairo2 libfontconfig1 libgdk-pixbuf2.0-0
  libgdk-pixbuf2.0-common libjbig0 libjpeg-turbo8 libjpeg8 libjs-jquery libjs-prototype libjs-scriptaculous
  libpixman-1-0 libtiff5 libx11-6 libx11-data libxau6 libxcb-render0 libxcb-shm0 libxcb1 libxdmcp6 libxext6
  libxrender1 python-attr python-cairo python-cffi-backend python-cryptography python-django python-django-common
  python-django-tagging python-enum34 python-idna python-ipaddress python-openssl python-pam python-pyasn1
  python-pyasn1-modules python-pyparsing python-serial python-service-identity python-simplejson python-sqlparse
  python-twisted-bin python-twisted-core python-tz python-whisper python-zope.interface python3-cairocffi python3-cffi
  python3-cffi-backend python3-cryptography python3-flask python3-idna python3-itsdangerous python3-jinja2
  python3-markupsafe python3-openssl python3-ply python3-pyasn1 python3-pycparser python3-pyinotify python3-pyparsing
  python3-structlog python3-tz python3-tzlocal python3-werkzeug python3-xcffib python3-yaml
```

Edit the storage schemas file /etc/graphite/storage-schemas.conf and place the following into it:

```
[carbon]
pattern = ^carbon\.
retentions = 60:90d
[default_1min_for_1day]
pattern = .*
retentions = 60s:1d
```

And now we can create the graphite database by running the following command:

```
sudo graphite-manage syncdb
```

The preceding command will give the following output:

```
You have installed Django's auth system, and don't have any superusers defined.
Would you like to create one now? (yes/no): yes
Username (leave blank to use 'root'):
Email address:
Password:
Password (again):
Superuser created successfully.
```

Set the password for the root user when prompted:

```
sudo apt-get install apache2 libapache2-mod-wsgi
```

The preceding command gives the following output:

```
vagrant@ansible:~$ sudo apt-get install apache2 libapache2-mod-wsgi
Reading package lists... Done
Building dependency tree
Reading state information... Done
The following additional packages will be installed:
  apache2-bin apache2-data apache2-utils libaprutil1-dbd-sqlite3 libaprutil1-ldap liblua5.1-0 libpython2.7 ssl-cert
Suggested packages:
  www-browser apache2-doc apache2-suexec-pristine | apache2-suexec-custom openssl-blacklist
The following NEW packages will be installed:
  apache2 apache2-bin apache2-data apache2-utils libapache2-mod-wsgi libaprutil1-dbd-sqlite3 libaprutil1-ldap
  liblua5.1-0 libpython2.7 ssl-cert
0 upgraded, 10 newly installed, 0 to remove and 122 not upgraded.
Need to get 2,538 kB of archives.
After this operation, 9,814 kB of additional disk space will be used.
Do you want to continue? [Y/n]
```

In order to stop the default apache site from conflicting with the graphite web service, we need to disable it by running the following command:

```
sudo a2dissite 000-default
```

The preceding command gives the following output:

```
vagrant@ansible:~$ sudo a2dissite 000-default
Site 000-default disabled.
To activate the new configuration, you need to run:
  service apache2 reload
vagrant@ansible:~$
```

We can now copy the apache graphite configuration into the apache environment:

```
sudo cp /usr/share/graphite-web/apache2-graphite.conf
/etc/apache2/sites-available
sudo a2ensite apache2-graphite
```

The preceding commands give the following output:

```
vagrant@ansible:~$ sudo a2ensite apache2-graphite
Enabling site apache2-graphite.
To activate the new configuration, you need to run:
  service apache2 reload
vagrant@ansible:~$
```

Restart the apache service:

```
sudo service apache2 reload
```

Grafana

We will edit the apt repository file and add the repository for grafana:

```
sudo nano /etc/apt/sources.list.d/grafana.list
```

Place the following line into the file and save it:

```
deb https://packagecloud.io/grafana/stable/debian/ jessie main
```

And now run the following commands to retrieve the gpg key and update the package lists:

```
curl https://packagecloud.io/gpg.key | sudo apt-key add -
sudo apt-get update
```

Install Grafana using the following command:

```
sudo apt-get install grafana
```

The preceding command gives the following output:

```
vagrant@ansible:~$ sudo apt-get install grafana
Reading package lists... Done
Building dependency tree
Reading state information... Done
The following additional packages will be installed:
  build-essential dpkg-dev fonts-font-awesome g++ g++-5 golang-1.6-go golang-1.6-race-detector-runtime golang-1.6-src
  golang-go golang-race-detector-runtime golang-src grafana-data libalgorithm-diff-perl libalgorithm-diff-xs-perl
  libalgorithm-merge-perl libjs-angularjs libjs-jquery-metadata libjs-jquery-tablesorter libjs-twitter-bootstrap
  libstdc++-5-dev pkg-config
Suggested packages:
  debian-keyring g++-multilib g++-5-multilib gcc-5-doc libstdc++6-5-dbg bzr mercurial libjs-bootstrap libstdc++-5-doc
The following NEW packages will be installed:
  build-essential dpkg-dev fonts-font-awesome g++ g++-5 golang-1.6-go golang-1.6-race-detector-runtime golang-1.6-src
  golang-go golang-race-detector-runtime golang-src grafana grafana-data libalgorithm-diff-perl
  libalgorithm-diff-xs-perl libalgorithm-merge-perl libjs-angularjs libjs-jquery-metadata libjs-jquery-tablesorter
  libjs-twitter-bootstrap libstdc++-5-dev pkg-config
0 upgraded, 22 newly installed, 0 to remove and 122 not upgraded.
Need to get 43.1 MB of archives.
After this operation, 268 MB of additional disk space will be used.
Do you want to continue? [Y/n]
```

With the standard Vagrant configuration, you will not be able to connect to the HTTP port provided by Grafana. To access Grafana, we will need to port forward via ssh port 3000 to our local machine.

An example using PuTTY is shown in the following screenshot:

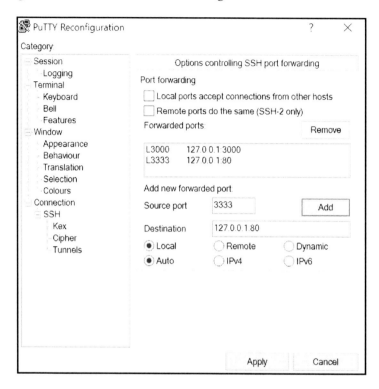

Now use `http://localhost:3000` in the URL, and you should be taken to the Grafana home page. Navigate to data sources and then let's configure Grafana to poll our newly installed Graphite installation:

If you get the green success bar when you click on the **Save & Test** button, then you have successfully installed and configured Graphite and Grafana.

collectd

Now that we have a shiny installation of Graphite and Grafana to look at, we need to put some data into it to be able to generate some graphs. collectd is a well respected metric collection tool, which can output metrics to Graphite. The core collectd application is very minimal, and it relies on a series of plugins to collect metrics and forwards them onto applications such as Graphite for storage.

Before we start collecting metrics from our Ceph nodes, let's install collectd on the same VM as where we installed Graphite and Grafana. We will do this to gain a better understanding of collectd and the process required to configure it. We will then use Ansible to install and configure collectd on all of our Ceph nodes, which would be the recommended approach if this was being rolled out in a production environment. We have the following code:

```
sudo apt-get install collectd-core
```

The preceding command will give the following output:

```
vagrant@ansible:~$ sudo apt-get install collectd-core
Reading package lists... Done
Building dependency tree
Reading state information... Done
The following additional packages will be installed:
  fontconfig libdatrie1 libdbi1 libgraphite2-3 libharfbuzz0b libltdl7 libpango-1.0-0 libpangocairo-1.0-0
  libpangoft2-1.0-0 librrd4 libthai-data libthai0 rrdtool
Suggested packages:
  collectd-dev librrds-perl liburi-perl libhtml-parser-perl libregexp-common-perl libconfig-general-perl
  apcupsd bind9 hddtemp ipvsadm lm-sensors mbmon memcached mysql-server | virtual-mysql-server nginx
  notification-daemon nut openvpn olsrd pdns-server postgresql redis-server slapd time-daemon varnish
  zookeeper libatasmart4 libesmtp6 libganglia1 libhiredis0.13 libmemcached11 libmodbus5 libmysqlclient20
  libnotify4 libopenipmi0 liboping0 libowcapi-3.1-1 libpq5 libprotobuf-c1 librabbitmq4 librdkafka1
  libsensors4 libsigrok2 libsnmp30 libtokyotyrant3 libupsclient4 libvarnishapi1 libvirt0 libyajl2
  default-jre-headless
The following NEW packages will be installed:
  collectd-core fontconfig libdatrie1 libdbi1 libgraphite2-3 libharfbuzz0b libltdl7 libpango-1.0-0
  libpangocairo-1.0-0 libpangoft2-1.0-0 librrd4 libthai-data libthai0 rrdtool
0 upgraded, 14 newly installed, 0 to remove and 122 not upgraded.
Need to get 2,193 kB of archives.
After this operation, 8,419 kB of additional disk space will be used.
Do you want to continue? [Y/n]
```

This will install collectd and a basic set of plugins for querying standard operating system resources. There is a sample configuration stored in the following location:

```
/usr/share/doc/collectd-core/examples/collectd.conf
```

It lists all of the core plugins and sample configuration options. It is worth reviewing this file to learn about the various plugins and their configuration options. For this example, however, we will start with an empty configuration file and configure a few basic resources:

1. Create a new `collectd` configuration file using the following command:

```
sudo nano /etc/collectd/collectd.conf
```

2. Add the following in it:

```
Hostname "ansible"

LoadPlugin cpu
LoadPlugin df
LoadPlugin load
```

```
LoadPlugin memory
LoadPlugin write_graphite

<Plugin write_graphite>
   <Node "graphing">
       Host "localhost"
       Port "2003"
       Protocol "tcp"
       LogSendErrors true
       Prefix "collectd."
       StoreRates true
       AlwaysAppendDS false
       EscapeCharacter "_"
   </Node>
</Plugin>

<Plugin "df">
  FSType "ext4"
</Plugin>
```

3. Restart the `collectd` service using the following command:

   `sudo service collectd restart`

4. Now navigate back to Grafana and browse the dashboards menu item. Click on the button in the middle of the screen to create a new dashboard:

5. Select **Graph** to add a new graph to the dashboard. An example graph will now appear, which we will want to edit to replace with our own graphs. To do this, click on the graph title and a floating menu will appear:

6. Click on **Edit** to go to the graph widget editing screen. From here, we can delete the fake graph data by selecting the *dustbin* icon, as shown in the following three-button menu box:

7. Now from the drop-down menu, change the panel data source to the graphite source we have just added and click on the `Add query` button.

8. A query box will appear at the top of the editing panel, it will also have the three-button menu box like before. From here, we can toggle the edit mode of the query editor by clicking on the button with the three horizontal lines:

The **Toggle Edit Mode** option switches the query editor between click and select mode, where you can explore the available metrics and build up basic queries and the text editor mode. The click and select mode is useful if you do not know the names of the metrics and only want to create basic queries. For more advanced queries, the text editor is required.

We will first make a query for our graph using the basic editor mode and then switch to the text mode for the rest of this chapter to make it easier to copy the queries from this book.

Let's first graph the system load of VM where we have installed collectd:

It will now produce a graph given earlier, showing the system load.

By further clicking on the + symbol, you can expand the query by applying different functions against the data. These could be used to add multiple data sources together or to find the average. We will cover this further in the chapter as we begin to craft some queries to analyze Ceph performance. Before we continue, let's now switch the query editor mode to the text mode to see what the query looks like:

You can see that each leaf of the tree of metrics is separated by a dot. This is how the Graphite query language works.

Deploying collectd with Ansible

Now that we have confirmed that our monitoring stack is installed and working correctly. Let's use Ansible to deploy collectd to all our Ceph nodes, so we can start monitoring it.

Switch to the `ansible` directory:

```
cd /etc/ansible/roles
git clone https://github.com/fiskn/Stouts.collectd
```

Edit your Ansible `site.yml` file and add the `collectd` role to the plays for your `mon` and `osd` nodes so that they look like the following:

```
- hosts: mons
  gather_facts: false
  become: True
  roles:
  - ceph-mon
  - Stouts.collectd
```

Edit `group_vars/all` to enter the following:

```
collectd_use_ppa: yes
collectd_use_ppa_latest: yes
collectd_ppa_source: 'deb http://pkg.ci.collectd.org/deb xenial collectd-5.7'

collectd_write_graphite: yes
collectd_write_graphite_options:
  Host: "ansible"
  Port: 2003
  Prefix: collectd.
  # Postfix: .collectd
  Protocol: tcp
  AlwaysAppendDS: false
  EscapeCharacter: _
  LogSendErrors: true
  StoreRates: true
  SeparateInstances: true
  PreserveSeparator: true

collectd_ceph: yes
```

Now run your `site.yml` playbook:

```
ansible-playbook -K site.yml
```

The preceding command gives the following output:

```
RUNNING HANDLER [Stouts.collectd : collectd restart] ****************************
changed: [osd2]
changed: [osd3]
changed: [osd1]

PLAY RECAP **********************************************************************
mon1                       : ok=67    changed=8    unreachable=0    failed=0
mon2                       : ok=61    changed=6    unreachable=0    failed=0
mon3                       : ok=61    changed=6    unreachable=0    failed=0
osd1                       : ok=65    changed=6    unreachable=0    failed=0
osd2                       : ok=63    changed=6    unreachable=0    failed=0
osd3                       : ok=63    changed=6    unreachable=0    failed=0
```

You should see from the status at the end, that Ansible has deployed collectd to all your Ceph nodes, and it has configured the collectd Ceph plugin. In Grafana, you should now be able to see your Ceph nodes showing up as available metrics. The following is one of our monitor nodes:

For example, we can now create a graph showing the number objects stored in the Ceph cluster. Create a new graph in Grafana and enter the following query:

```
collectd.mon1.ceph.mon.mon1.ceph_bytes.Cluster.numObject
```

This will produce a graph like the following:

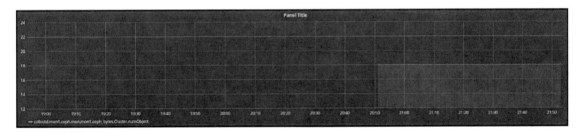

It's advised that you spend some time browsing through the available metrics so that you are familiar with them before proceeding to the next section.

Sample Graphite queries for Ceph

Although you can generate some very useful graphs by simply selecting individual metrics, by harnessing the power of Graphite's functions to manipulate the metrics, graphs can be created, which offer a much more detailed insight into your Ceph cluster. The following Graphite queries are useful for generating common graphs and are also a good starting point to create your own custom queries.

Number of Up and In OSDs

It's very handy to be able to quickly glance at a dashboard and see how many OSDs are Up and In. The following two queries show these values:

```
maxSeries(collectd.mon*.ceph.mon.mon*.ceph_bytes.Cluster.numOsdIn)
```

```
maxSeries(collectd.mon*.ceph.mon.mon*.ceph_bytes.Cluster.numOsdUp)
```

Note the use of the maxSeries function, which allows data to be pulled from all the mon nodes and will take the highest value.

Showing most deviant OSD usage

Due to the way CRUSH places PGs on each OSD, there will never be a perfect balance of PGs per OSD. The following query will create a graph that will show the 10 most deviant OSDs, so you can see if PG balancing would be beneficial. We have the following code:

```
mostDeviant(10,collectd.osd*.df.var-lib-ceph-osd-ceph-
*.df_complex.used)
```

Total number of IOPs across all OSDs

This uses the sumSeries function and wildcards to add together all the op metrics from every OSD:

```
sumSeries(collectd.osd*.ceph.osd.*.ceph_rate.Osd.op)
```

There are also counters that will show read and write operations individually, named opR and opW, respectively.

Total MBps across all OSDs

Similarly, there are also counters that show MBps for each OSD, such as the op counters; the sumSeries function can also be used. We have the following code:

```
sumSeries(collectd.osd*.ceph.osd.*.ceph_rate.Osd.{opInBytes,opOutBy
tes})
```

Cluster capacity and usage

The following two queries show the total capacity of bytes in the cluster and the number of bytes used. They can be used to generate pie chart in Grafana to show the percentage of used space. Note that these counters show the raw capacity before replication:

```
maxSeries(collectd.mon*.ceph.mon.mon*.ceph_bytes.Cluster.osdBytes)

maxSeries(collectd.mon*.ceph.mon.mon*.ceph_bytes.Cluster.osdBytesUsed)
```

Average latency

The following two queries can be used to graph the average latency of the cluster. Larger I/O sizes per operation will increase the average latency, as larger I/Os take longer to process. As such, these graphs will not give a clear picture of your clusters latency if average I/O size changes over time. We have the following code:

```
averageSeries(collectd.osd*.ceph.osd.*.ceph_latency.Osd.opWLatency)

averageSeries(collectd.osd*.ceph.osd.*.ceph_latency.Osd.opRLatency)
```

Custom Ceph collectd plugins

Although the standard collectd Ceph plugin does a good job of collecting all of Ceph's performance counters, it falls short of collecting all the required data to allow you to get a complete view of your cluster health and performance. This section will demonstrate how to use additional custom collectd plugins to collect the PG states, per pool performance stats, and more realistic latency figures:

1. Jump on to one of your mon nodes via SSH and clone the following git repository:

   ```
   git clone https://github.com/grinapo/collectd-ceph
   ```

2. Create a ceph directory under the collectd/plugins directory:

   ```
   sudo mkdir -p /usr/lib/collectd/plugins/ceph
   ```

3. Copy the `plugins` directory to `/usr/lib/collectd/plugins/ceph` using the following command:

```
sudo cp -a collectd-ceph/plugins/*
/usr/lib/collectd/plugins/ceph/
```

4. Now create a new `collectd` configuration file to enable the plugins:

```
sudo nano /etc/collectd/collectd.conf.d/ceph2.conf
```

5. Place the following configuration inside it and save the new file:

```
<LoadPlugin "python">
    Globals true
</LoadPlugin>

<Plugin "python">
    ModulePath "/usr/lib/collectd/plugins/ceph"

    Import "ceph_pool_plugin"
    Import "ceph_pg_plugin"
    Import "ceph_latency_plugin"

    <Module "ceph_pool_plugin">
        Verbose "True"
        Cluster "ceph"
        Interval "60"
    </Module>
    <Module "ceph_pg_plugin">
        Verbose "True"
        Cluster "ceph"
        Interval "60"
    </Module>
    <Module "ceph_latency_plugin">
        Verbose "True"
        Cluster "ceph"
        Interval "60"
        TestPool "rbd"
    </Module>
</Plugin>
```

The latency plugin uses RADOS bench to determine the cluster latency; this means that it is actually running RADOS bench and will write data to your cluster. The `TestPool` parameter determines the target for the RADOS bench command. It is therefore recommended that on a production cluster, a separate small pool is created for this use.

 If you are trying to use these extra plugins on Kraken+ releases of Ceph, you will need to edit the `ceph_pg_plugin.py` file and modify the variable name on line 71 from `fs_perf_stat` to `perf_stat`.

6. Restart the `collectd` service:

```
service collectd restart
```

The average cluster latency can now be obtained by the following query:

```
collectd.mon1.ceph-ceph.cluster.gauge.avg_latency
```

This figure is based on doing 64 Kb writes, and so unlike the OSD metrics, it will not change depending on the average client I/O size.

Summary

In this chapter, you learned the importance of monitoring your Ceph cluster and its supporting infrastructure. You should also have a good understanding of the various components that you should monitor and some example tools that can be used. We covered some of the PG states that in conjunction with a monitoring solution will allow you to understand the current status of your Ceph cluster. Finally, we deployed a highly scalable monitoring system comprising collectd, Graphite, and Grafana, which will enable you to create professional looking dashboards to show the status and performance of your Ceph cluster.

8
Tiering with Ceph

The tiering functionality in Ceph allows you to overlay one RADOS pool over another and let Ceph intelligently promote and evict objects between them. In most configurations, the top-level pool will be comprised of fast storage devices like **Solid State Drives (SSDs)** and the base pool will be comprised of the slower storage devices like **Serial ATA (SATA)** or **Serial Attached SCSI (SAS)** disks. If the working set of your data is of a comparatively small percentage, then this allows you to use Ceph to provide high capacity storage but yet still maintain a good level of performance of frequently accessed data.

In this chapter, we will cover the following topics:

- How Cephs tiering functionality works
- What are good use cases for tiering
- How to configure two pools into a tier
- Cover various tuning options available for tiering

 It's recommended that you should be running at least the Jewel release of Ceph if you wish to use the tiering functionality. Previous releases were lacking a lot of required features that made tiering usable.

Tiering versus caching

Although often described as **cache tiering**, it's better to think of the functionality in Ceph as a tiering technology rather than a cache. It's important that you take this into consideration before reading any further as it's vital to understand the difference between the two.

A cache is typically designed to accelerate access to a set of data unless it's a writeback cache; it will not hold the only copy of the data, and normally there is little overhead to promoting data to cache. Cache tends to operate over a shorter timeframe, quite often everything that is accessed is promoted into cache.

A tiering solution is also designed to accelerate access to a set of data; however, it's promotion strategy normally works over a longer period of time and is more selective about what data is promoted, mainly due to the promotion action having a small impact on overall storage performance. Also, it is quite common with tiering technologies that only a single tier may hold the valid state of the data, and so all tiers in the system need equal protection against data loss.

How Cephs tiering functionality works

Once you have configured a RADOS pool to be an overlay of another RADOS pool, Cephs tiering functionality works on the basic principal that if an object does not exist in the top-level tier, then it must exist in the base tier. All object requests from clients are sent to the top tier; if the OSD does not have the requested object, then depending on the tiering mode, it may either proxy the read or write request down to the base tier or force a promotion. The base tier then proxies the request back through the top tier to the client. It's important to note that the tiering functionality is transparent to clients, and there is no specific client configuration needed.

There are three main actions in tiering that move objects between tiers. **Promotions** copy objects from the base tier up to the top tier. If tiering is configured in writeback mode, the **flushing** action is used to update the contents of the base tier object from the top tier. Finally, when the top tier pool reaches capacity, objects are evicted by the **eviction** action.

In order to be able to make decisions on what objects to move between the two tiers, Ceph uses HitSets to track accesses to objects. A **HitSet** is a collection of all object access requests and is consulted to determine if an object has had either a read or write request since that HitSet was created. The HitSets use a **bloom filter** to statistically track object accesses rather than storing every access to every object, which would generate large overheads. The bloom filter only stores binary states; an object can only be marked as accessed or not; and there is no concept of storing the number of accesses to an object in a single HitSet. If an object appears in a number of the most recent HitSets and is in the base pool, then it will be promoted.

Likewise, objects that no longer appear in recent HitSets will become candidates for flushing or eviction if the top tier comes under pressure. The number of HitSets and how often a new one gets created can be configured, along with the required number of recent HitSets a write or read I/O must appear in, in order for a promotion to take place. The size of the top-level tier can also be configured and is disconnected from the available capacity of the RADOS pool it sits on.

There are a number of configuration and tuning options that define how Ceph reacts to the generated HitSets and the thresholds at which promotions, flushes, and evictions occur. These will be covered in more detail later in the chapter.

What is a bloom filter

A bloom filter is used in Ceph to provide an efficient way of tracking whether an object is a member of a HitSet without having to individually store the access status of each object. It is probabilistic in nature, and although it can return **false positives**, it will never return as **false negative**. This means that when querying a bloom filter, it may report that an item is present when it is not, but it will never report that an item is not present when it is.

Ceph's use of bloom filters allows it to efficiently track the accesses of millions of objects without the overhead of storing every single access. In the event of a false positive, it could mean that an object is incorrectly promoted; however, the probability of this happening combined with the minimal impact is of little concern.

Tiering modes

There are a number of tiering modes that determine the precise actions of how Ceph reacts to the contents of the HitSets. However, in most cases, the writeback mode will be used. The available modes for use in tiering are **writeback**, **forward**, **read-forward**, **proxy**, and **read-proxy**. There are brief descriptions of the available modes and how they act.

Writeback

In writeback mode, data is promoted to the top-level tier by both reads and writes depending on how frequently accessed the object are. Objects in the top-level tier can be modified, and dirty objects will be flushed to the pool at a later date. If an object needs to be read or written to in the bottom tier and the bottom pool supports it, then Ceph will try and directly proxy the operation that has a minimal impact on latency.

Forward

The forward mode simply forwards all requests from the top tier to the base tier without doing any promotions. It should be noted that a forward causes OSD to tell the client to resend the request to the correct OSD and so has a greater impact on latency than just simply proxying it.

Read-forward

Read-forward mode forces a promotion on every write and like the forward mode earlier, redirects the client for all reads to the base pool. This can be useful if you wish to only use the top-tier pool for write acceleration. Using write intensive SSDs overlayed over read intensive SSDs is one such example.

Proxy

Similar to forward mode, except proxy all reads and writes without promoting anything. By proxying the request, OSD itself retrieves data from the base tier OSD and then passes it back to the client. This reduces the overhead compared with using forwarding.

Read-proxy

Similar to read-forward mode, except that it proxies reads and always promote on writes requests. It should be noted that the writeback and read-proxy modes are the only modes that receive rigorous testing, and so care should be taken when using the other modes. Also, there is probably little gain from using the other modes, and they will likely be phased out in future releases.

Uses cases

As mentioned at the start of the chapter, the tiering functionality should be thought of as tiering and not a cache. The reason behind this statement is that the act of promotions has a detrimental effect to cluster performance when compared with most caching solutions, which do normally not degrade performance if enabled on noncacheable workloads. The performance impact of promotions are caused by two main reasons. First, the promotion happens in the I/O path, the entire object to be promoted needs to be read from the base tier and then written into the top tier before the I/O is returned to the client.

Second, this promotion action will likely also cause a flush and an eviction, which cause even more reads and writes to both tiers. If both tiers are using 3x replication, this starts to cause a large amount of write amplification for even just a single promotion. In the worse case scenario, a single 4 KB access that causes a promotion could cause 8 MB of read I/O and 24 MB of write I/O across the two tiers. This increased I/O will cause an increase in latency; for this reason, promotions should be considered expensive, and tuning should be done to minimize them.

With that in mind, Ceph tiering should only be used where the hot or active part of the data will fit into the top tier. Workloads that are uniformly random will likely see no benefit and in many cases may actually cause a performance degradation, either due to no suitable objects being available to promote, or too many promotions occurring.

Most workloads that involve providing storage for generic virtual machines tend to be good candidates as normally only a small percentage of VM tends to be accessed.

Online transaction processing (OLTP) databases, will normally show improvements when used with either caching or tiering as their hot set of data is relatively small and data patterns are reasonably consistent. However, reporting or batch processing database are generally not a good fit as they can quite often require a large range of the data to be accessed without any prior warm up period.

RADOS Block Devices (RBD) workloads that involve random access with no specific pattern or workloads that involve large read or write streaming should be avoided and will likely suffer from the addition of a cache tier.

Creating tiers in Ceph

To test Ceph tiering functionality, two RADOS pools are required. If you are running these examples on a laptop or desktop hardware, although spinning disk-based OSDs can be used to create the pools; SSDs are highly recommended if there is any intention to read and write data. If you have multiple disk types available in your testing hardware, then the base tier can exist on spinning disks and the top tier can be placed on SSDs.

Let's create tiers using the following commands, all of which make use of the Ceph `tier` command:

1. Create two RADOS pools:

    ```
    ceph osd pool create base 64 64 replicated

    ceph osd pool create top 64 64 replicated
    ```

    The preceding commands give the following output:

    ```
    root@mon1:/home/vagrant# ceph osd pool create base 64 64 replicated
    pool 'base' created
    root@mon1:/home/vagrant# ceph osd pool create top 64 64 replicated
    pool 'top' created
    ```

2. Create a tier consisting of the two pools:

    ```
    ceph osd tier add base top
    ```

    The preceding command gives the following output:

    ```
    root@mon1:/home/vagrant# ceph osd tier add base top
    pool 'top' is now (or already was) a tier of 'base'
    ```

3. Configure the cache mode:

    ```
    ceph osd tier cache-mode top writeback
    ```

    The preceding command gives the following output:

    ```
    root@mon1:/home/vagrant# ceph osd tier cache-mode top writeback
    set cache-mode for pool 'top' to writeback
    ```

4. Make the top tier and overlay of the base tier:

    ```
    ceph osd tier set-overlay base top
    ```

    The preceding command gives the following output:

    ```
    root@mon1:/home/vagrant# ceph osd tier set-overlay base top
    overlay for 'base' is now (or already was) 'top'
    ```

5. Now that the tiering is configured, we need to set some simple values to make sure that the tiering agent can function. Without these, the tiering mechanism will not work properly. Note that these commands are just setting variables on the pool:

```
ceph osd pool set top hit_set_type bloom

ceph osd pool set top hit_set_count 10

ceph osd pool set top hit_set_period 60

ceph osd pool set top target_max_bytes 100000000
```

The preceding commands give the following output:

```
root@mon1:/home/vagrant# ceph osd pool set top hit_set_type bloom
set pool 5 hit_set_type to bloom
root@mon1:/home/vagrant# ceph osd pool set top hit_set_count 10
set pool 5 hit_set_count to 10
root@mon1:/home/vagrant# ceph osd pool set top hit_set_period 60
set pool 5 hit_set_period to 60
root@mon1:/home/vagrant# ceph osd pool set top target_max_bytes 100000000
set pool 5 target_max_bytes to 100000000
```

The earlier-mentioned commands are simply telling Ceph that the HitSets should be created using the bloom filter. It should create a new HitSet every 60 seconds and that it should keep 10 of them before discarding the oldest one. Finally, the top tier pool should hold no more than 100 MB; if it reaches this limit, I/O operations will block. More detailed explanations of these settings will follow in the next section.

6. Next, we need to configure the various options that control how Ceph flushes and evicts objects from the top to the base tier:

```
ceph osd pool set top cache_target_dirty_ratio 0.4

ceph osd pool set top cache_target_full_ratio 0.8
```

The preceding commands give the following output:

```
root@mon1:/home/vagrant# ceph osd pool set top cache_target_dirty_ratio 0.4
set pool 5 cache_target_dirty_ratio to 0.4
root@mon1:/home/vagrant# ceph osd pool set top cache_target_full_ratio 0.8
set pool 5 cache_target_full_ratio to 0.8
```

The earlier example tells Ceph that it should start flushing dirty objects in the top tier down to the base tier when the top tier is 40% full. And that objects should be evicted from the top tier when the top tier is 80% full.

7. And finally the last two commands instruct Ceph that any object should have been in the top tier for at least 60 seconds before it can be considered for flushing or eviction:

```
ceph osd pool set top cache_min_flush_age 60

ceph osd pool set top cache_min_evict_age 60
```

The preceding commands give the following output:

```
root@mon1:/home/vagrant# ceph osd pool set top cache_min_flush_age 60
set pool 5 cache_min_flush_age to 60
root@mon1:/home/vagrant# ceph osd pool set top cache_min_evict_age 60
set pool 5 cache_min_evict_age to 60
```

Tuning tiering

Unlike the majority of Cephs features, which by default perform well for a large number of workloads, Cephs tiering functionality requires carefully configuration of its various parameters to ensure good performance. You should also have a basic understanding of your workloads I/O profile; tiering will only work well if your data has a small percentage of hot data. Workloads that are uniformly random or involve lots of sequential access patterns will either show no improvement or in some cases may actually be slower.

Flushing and eviction

The main tuning options should be looked at first are the ones that define the size limit to the top tier, when it should flush and when it should evict.

The following two configuration options configure the maximum size of the data to be stored in the top tier pool:

```
target_max_bytes

target_max_objects
```

The size is either specified in bytes or number objects and does not have to be the same size as the actual pool, but it cannot be larger. The size is also based on the available capacity after replication of the RADOS pool, so for a 3x replica pool, this will be a one-third of your raw capacity. If the number of bytes or objects in this pool goes above this limit, I/O will block; therefore, it's important that thought is given to the other config options later so that this limit is not reached. It's also important that this value is set, as without it, no flushing or evictions will occur and the pool will simply fill up OSDs to their full limit and then block I/O.

The reason that this setting exists instead of Ceph just using the size of the underlying capacity of the disks in the RADOS pool is that by specifying the size, you could if you desire, have multiple top-level tier pools on the same set of disks.

As you have learned earlier, `target_max_bytes` sets the maximum size of the tiered data on the pool and if this limit is reached, I/O will block. In order to make sure that the RADOS pool does not reach this limit, `cache_target_full_ratio` instructs Ceph to try and keep the pool at a percentage of `target_max_bytes` by evicting objects when this target is breached. Unlike promotions and flushes, evictions are fairly low-cost operations:

```
cache_target_full_ratio
```

The value is specified as a value between `0` and `1` and works like a percentage. It should be noted that although `target_max_bytes` and `cache_target_full_ratio` are set against the pool, internally Ceph uses these values to calculate per PG limits instead. This can mean that in certain circumstances, some PGs may reach the calculated maximum limit before others and can sometimes lead to unexpected results. For this reason, it is recommended not to set `cache_target_full_ratio` to high and leave some headroom; a value of 0.8 normally works well. We have the following code:

```
cache_target_dirty_ratio
```

```
cache_target_dirty_high_ratio
```

These two configuration options control when Ceph flushes dirty objects from the top tier to the base tier if the tiering has been configured in writeback mode. An object is considered dirty if it has been modified while being in the top tier, objects modified in the base tier do not get marked as dirty. Flushing involves copying the object out of the top tier and into the base tier, as this is a full object write, the base tier can be an erasure-coded pool. The behavior is asynchronous and aside from increasing I/O on the RADOS pools, is not directly linked to any impact on client I/O. Objects are typically flushed at a lower speed than what they can be evicted at. As flushing is an expensive operation compared with eviction, this means that if required, large amounts of objects can be evicted quickly if needed.

The two ratios control what speed of flushing OSD allows, by restricting the number of parallel flushing threads that are allowed to run at once. These can be controlled by the OSD configuration options `osd_agent_max_ops` and `osd_agent_max_high_ops`, respectively. By default, these are set to 2 and 4 parallel threads.

In theory, the percentage of dirty objects should hover around the low dirty ratio during normal cluster usage. This will mean that objects are flushed with a low parallelism of flushing to minimize the impact on cluster latency. As normal bursts of writes hit the cluster, the number of dirty objects may rise, but over time, these writes are flushed down to the base tier.

However, if there are periods of sustained writes that outstrip the low speed flushing's capability, then the number of dirty objects will start to rise. Hopefully, this period of high write I/O will not go on for long enough to fill the tier with dirty objects and thus will gradually reduce back down to the low threshold. However, if the number of dirty objects continues to increase and reaches the high ratio, then the flushing parallelism gets increased and will hopefully be able to stop the number of dirty objects from increasing any further. Once the write traffic reduces, the number of dirty objects will be brought back down the low ratio again. These sequence of events are illustrated in the following graph:

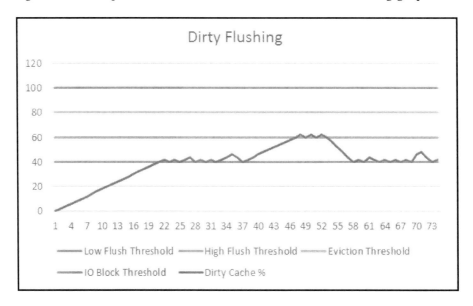

The two dirty ratios should have sufficient difference between them that normal bursts of writes can be absorbed, without the high ratio kicking in. The high ratio should be thought of as an emergency limit. A good value to start with is 0.4 for the low ratio and 0.6 for the high ratio.

The `osd_agent_max_ops` configuration settings should be adjusted so that in normal operating conditions, the number of dirty objects is hovering around or just over the low dirty ratio. It's not easy to recommend a value for these settings as they will largely depend on the ratio of the size and performance of the top tier to the base tier. However, start with setting `osd_agent_max_ops` to 1 and increase as necessary and set `osd_agent_max_high_ops` to at least double.

If you see status messages in the Ceph status screen indicating that high-speed flushing is occurring, then you will want to increase `osd_agent_max_ops`. If you ever see the top tier getting full and blocking I/O, then you either need to consider lowering the `cache_target_dirty_high_ratio` variable or increase the `osd_agent_max_high_ops` setting to stop the tier filling up with dirty objects.

Promotions

The next tuning options that should be looked at are the ones that define the HitSets and the required recency to trigger a promotion:

> `hitset_count`

> `hitset_period`

The `hitset_count` setting controls how many HitSets can exist before the oldest one starts getting trimmed. The `hitset_period` setting controls how often a HitSet should be created. If you are testing tiering in a laboratory environment, it should be noted that I/O to the PG needs to be occurring in order for a HitSet to be created; on an idle cluster, no HitSets will be created or trimmed.

Having the correct number and controlling how often HitSets are created is a key to being able to reliably control when objects get promoted. Remember that HitSets only contain data about whether an object has been accessed or not; they don't contain a count of the number of times an object was accessed. If `hitset_period` is too large, then even relatively low-accessed objects will appear in the majority of the HitSets. For example, with a `hitset_period` of 2 minutes, an RBD object containing the disk block where a log file is updated once a minute would be in all the same HitSets as an object getting access 100 times a second.

Conversely, if the period is too low, then even hot objects may fail to appear in enough HitSets to make them candidates for promotion and your top tier will likely not be fully used. By finding the correct HitSet period, you should be able to capture the right view of your I/O that a suitable sized proportion of hot objects are candidates for promotion:

```
min_read_recency_for_promote
```

```
min_write_recency_for_promote
```

These two settings define how many of the last recent HitSets an object must appear in to be promoted. Due to the effect of probability, the relationship between semi-hot objects and recency setting is not linear. Once the recency settings are set past about 3 or 4, the number of eligible objects for promotion drops off in a logarithmic fashion. It should be noted that while promotion decisions can be made on reads or writes separately, they both reference the same HitSet data, which has no way of determining an access from being either a read or a write. As a handy feature, if you set the recency higher than the `hitset_count` setting, then it will never promote. This can be used for example to make sure that a write I/O will never cause an object to be promoted, by setting the write recency higher than the `hitset_count` setting.

Promotion throttling

As has been covered earlier, promotions are very expensive operations in tiering and care should be taken to make sure that they only happen when necessary. A large part of this is done by carefully tuning the HitSet and recency settings. However, in order to limit the impact of promotions, there is an additional throttle that restricts the number of promotions to a certain speed. This limit can either be specified as number of bytes or objects per second via two OSD configuration options:

```
osd_tier_promote_max_bytes_sec
```

```
osd_tier_promote_max_objects_sec
```

The default limits are 4 MBps or five objects a second. While these figures may sound low, especially when compared with the performance of the latest SSDs, their primary goal is to minimize the impact of promotions on latency. Careful tuning should be done to find a good balance on your cluster. It should be noted that this value is configured per OSD, and so the total promotion speed will be a sum across all OSDs.

Finally, the following configuration options allow tuning of the selection process for flushing objects:

```
hit_set_grade_search_last_n
```

This controls how may HitSets are queried in order to determine object temperature, with the the temperature of an object reflects how often it is accessed. A cold object is rarely accessed, with a hot object being accessed far more frequently being candidates for eviction. Setting this to a similar figure as the recency settings is recommended. We have the following code:

```
hit_set_grade_decay_rate
```

This works in combination with the `hit_set_grade_search_last_n` setting and decays the HitSet results the older they become. Objects that have been accessed more frequently than others have a hotter rating and will make sure that objects that are more frequently accessed are not incorrectly flushed. It should be noted that the `min_flush` and `evict_age` settings may override the temperature of an object when it comes to being flushed or evicted:

```
cache_min_flush_age
```

```
cache_min_evict_age
```

The `cache_min_evict_age` and `cache_min_flush_age` settings simply define how long an object must have not been modified for before it is allowed to be flushed or evicted. These can be used to stop objects that are only just not enough to be promoted, from continually being stuck in a cycle of moving between tiers. Setting them between 10 and 30 minutes is probably a good approach although care needs to be taken that the top tier does not fill up, in the case where there are no eligible objects to be flushed or evicted.

Monitoring parameters

In order to monitor the performance and characteristics of a cache tier in a Ceph cluster, there are a number of performance counters you can monitor. We will assume for the moment that you are already collecting the Ceph performance counters from the admin socket as discussed in the next chapter.

The most important thing to remember when looking at the performance counters is that once you configure a tier in Ceph all client requests, go through the top-level tier. Therefore, only read and write operation counters on OSDs that make up your top-level tier will show any requests, assuming that the base tier OSDs are not used for any other pools. To understand the number of requests handled by the base tier, there are proxy operation counters, which will show this number. These proxy operation counters are also calculated on the top-level OSDs, and so to monitor the throughput of a Ceph cluster with tiering, only the top-level OSDs need to be included in the calculations.

The following counters can be used to monitor tiering in Ceph, all are to be monitored on the top-level OSDs:

Counter	Description
op_r	Read operations handled by the OSD
op_w	Write operations handled by the OSD
tier_proxy_read	Read operations that were proxied to the base tier
tier_proxy_write	Write operations that were proxied to the base tier
tier_promote	The number of promotions from base to top-level tier
tier_try_flush	The number of flushes from the top-level to the base tier
tier_evict	The number of evictions from the top-level to the base tier

Tiering with erasure-coded pools

At the current time, Ceph doesn't support overwrite operations on erasure-coded pools and so cannot be directly used for storing RBD images. However, by the use of tiering, an erasure-coded pool can be used as the base pool and a 3x replica pool used as the top level. This allows the hot active dataset which will comprise of frequently accessed data, to sit in the top tier and any infrequently accessed cold data to reside in the base erasure-coded tier.

Care should be taken with this approach; although in theory it sounds like a brilliant idea, it shouldn't be forgotten that in this configuration proxy writes are not supported to the base erasure-coded pool. All write operations to the base tier therefore have to be promoted up to the top tier first. If even a small percentage write operations start targeting your base tier, then performance will quickly fall off a cliff as the constant promotion and flushing operations overwhelm the disks in your cluster. This approach is only recommended for use cases where write operations are infrequent or are contained to a small number of objects.

Alternative caching mechanisms

While the native RADOS tiering functionality provides numerous benefits around flexibility and allows management by the same Ceph toolset. However, it cannot be denied that for pure performance RADOS tiering lags behind other caching technologies that typically function at the block device level.

 Bcache is a block device cache in the Linux kernel, which can use a SSD to cache a slower block device such as a spinning disk.

Bcache is one example of a popular way of increasing the performance of Ceph with SSDs. Unlike RADOS tiering, which you can choose which pool you wish to cache, with bcache the entire OSD is cached. This method of caching brings a number of advantages around performance. The first is that the OSD itself has a much more consistent latency response due to the SSD caching. Filestore adds an increased amount of random I/O to every Ceph request regardless of whether the Ceph request is random of sequential in nature. Bcache can absorb these random I/Os and allow the spinning disk to perform a larger amount of sequential I/O. This can be very helpful during high periods of utilization where normal spinning disk OSDs would start to exhibit high latency. Second, where RADOS tiering operates at the size of the object stored in the pool, which is 4 MB by default for RBD workloads. Bcache caches data in much smaller blocks; this allows it to make better use of available SSD space and also suffer less from promotion overheads.

The SSD capacity assigned to bcache will also be used as a read cache for hot data; this will improve read performance as well as writes. Since bcache will only be using this capacity for read caching, it will only store one copy of the data and so will have 3x more read cache capacity than compared with using the same SSD in a RADOS-tiered pool.

However, there are a number of disadvantages to using bcache that make using RADOS cache pools still look attractive. As mentioned earlier, bcache will cache the entire OSD, in some cases where multiple pools may reside on the same OSDs, this behavior maybe undesirable. Also, once bcache has been configured with SSD and HDD, it is harder to expand the amount of cache if needed in the future. This also applies if your cluster does not currently have any form of caching; in this scenario, introducing bcache would be very disruptive. With RADOS tiering, you can simply add additional SSDs or specifically designed SSD nodes to add or expand the top tier as and when needed.

Another approach is to place the spinning disk OSDs behind a RAID controller with battery backed write back cache. The RAID controller performs a similar role to bcache and absorbs a lot of the random write I/O relating to filestore's extra metadata. Both latency and sequential write performance will increase as a result, read performance will unlikely increase however due to the relatively small size of the RAID controllers cache. Using a RAID controller, the OSD's journal can also be placed directly on the disk instead of using a separate SSD. By doing this, journal writes are absorbed by the RAID controllers cache and will improve the random performance of the journal, as likely most of the time, the journals contents will just be sitting in the controllers cache. Care does need to be taken though, as if the incoming write traffic exceeds the capacity of the controllers cache, journal contents will start being flushed to disk, and performance will degrade. For best performance a separate SSD or NVMe should be used for the filestore journal although attention should be paid to the cost of using both a RAID controller with sufficient performance and cache, in addition to the cost of the SSDs.

Both methods have their merits and should be considered before implementing caching in your cluster.

Summary

In this chapter, we have covered the theory behind Cephs RADOS tiering functionality and looked at the configuration and tuning operations available to best make it work for your workload. It should not be forgotten that the most important aspect is to understand your workload and be confident that its I/O pattern and distribution is cache friendly. By following the examples in this chapter, you should also now understand the required steps to implement tiered pools and how to apply the configuration options.

9
Tuning Ceph

While the default configuration of Linux and Ceph will likely provide reasonable performance due to many years of research and tweaking by developers, it is likely that a Ceph administrator may want to try and squeeze more performance out of its hardware. By tuning both, the operating system and Ceph, performance gains maybe realized. In the `Chapter 1`, *Planning for Ceph* you learned about how to choose hardware for a Ceph cluster; now let's learn how to make the most of it.

In this chapter, you will learn about the following topics:

- Latency and why it matters
- When you should tune
- The dangers of blindly setting configuration options
- The importance of benchmarks and when you should learn to ignore them
- The importance of being able to observe the results of your tuning
- Key tuning options that you should look at

It's important to understand that by tuning, all you are doing is reducing bottlenecks. If you manage to reduce enough bottlenecks in one area, the bottleneck will simply shift to another area. You will always have a bottleneck somewhere, and eventually, you will reach a point where you are simply overt the limit of what a particular hardware can provide. Therefore, the goal should be to reduce bottlenecks in the software and operating system to unlock the entire potential of your hardware.

Latency

When carrying out benchmarks, you are ultimately measuring the result of latency. All other forms of benchmarking metrics, including IOPS, MBps, or even higher level application metrics, are derived from the latency of that request.

IOPS are the number of I/O requests done in a second; the latency of each request directly effects the possible IOPS and can be seen by this formula:

$$IOP = \frac{1 \text{ Second}}{\text{Latency}} \text{ (in seconds)}$$

An average latency of 2 milliseconds per request will result in roughly 500 IOPS assuming each request is submitted in a synchronous fashion:

$$1/0.002 = 500$$

MBps is simply the number of IOPS multiplied by the I/O size:

$$500 \text{ IOPS} * 64 \text{ KB} = 32,000 \text{ KBps}$$

It should be clear that when you are carrying out benchmarks, you are actually measuring the end result of a latency. Therefore, any tuning that you are carrying out should be done to reduce end-to-end latency for each I/O request.

Before moving on to looking at how to benchmark various components of your Ceph cluster and the various tuning options available, we first need to understand the various sources of latency from a typical I/O request. Once we can break down each source of latency into its own category, then it will be possible to perform benchmarking on each one so that we can reliably track both negative and positive tuning outcomes at each stage.

The following diagram shows an example Ceph write request with the main sources of latency:

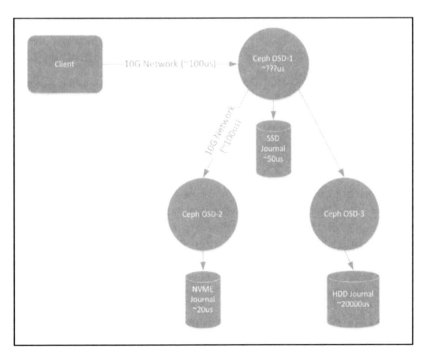

Starting with the client, we can see that on an average, there is probably around a 100 microseconds worth of latency for it to talk to the primary OSD. With 1G networking, this latency figure could be nearer to 1 milliseconds. We can confirm this figure by either using `ping` or `iperf` to measure the round trip delay between two nodes.

From the previous formula, we can see that with 1G networking, even if there were no other sources of latency, the maximum synchronous write IOPS would be around 1000.

Although the client introduces some latency of its own, it is minimal compared to the other sources, and so, it is not included in the diagram.

Next, the OSD which runs the Ceph code introduces latency as it processes the request. It is hard to put an exact figure against this, but it is affected by the speed of the CPU. A faster CPU with a higher frequency will run through the code path faster, reducing latency. Early on in the book, the primary OSD would send the request on to the other two OSDs in the replica set. These are both processed in parallel so that there is minimal increase in latency going from 2x to 3x replicas, assuming the backend disks can cope with the load.

There is also an extra network hop between the primary and the replicated OSDs, which introduces latency into each request

Once the primary OSD has committed the request to its journal and has had an acknowledgement back from all the replica OSDs that they have also done the same, it can then send an acknowledgment back to the client and can submit the next I/O request.

Regarding the journal, depending on the type of media being used, the commit latency can vary. NVMe SSDs will tend to service requests in the 10-20 microseconds range, whereas SATA/SAS based SSDs will typical service requests in the 50-100 microseconds range. NVMe devices also tend to have a more consistent latency profile with an increase in the queue depth, making them ideal for cases where multiple disks might use a single SSD as the same journal. Way ahead are the hard drives that are measured in 10s of milliseconds, although they are fairly consistent in terms of latency as the I/O size increases.

It should be obvious that for small, high-performance workloads, hard drive latency would dominate the total latency figures, and so, SSDs, preferably NVMe, should be used for it.

Overall, in a well-designed and tuned Ceph cluster, all of these parts combined should allow an average write 4 KB request to be serviced in around 500-750 microseconds.

Benchmarking

Benchmarking is an important tool to quickly be able to see the effect of your tuning efforts and also determine the limits of what your cluster is capable of. However, it's important that your benchmarks reflect the type of workload that you would be running normally on your Ceph cluster. It is pointless to tune your Ceph cluster to excel in large block sequential reads and writes if your final intention is to run highly latency sensitive OLTP databases on it. If possible, you should try and include some benchmarks that actually use the same software as your real-life workload. Again in the example of the OLTP database, look to see if there are benchmarks for your database software, which will give the most accurate results.

Benchmarking tools

The following list of tools are a recommended set of tools to get you started with benchmarking.

Fio

Fio, the flexible I/O testing tool, allows you to simulate a variety of complex I/O patterns through its extensive configuration options. It has plugins for both local block devices and RBD, meaning that you can test RBDs from your Ceph cluster either directly or by mounting them via the Linux RBD kernel driver.

Sysbench

Sysbench has a MySQL OLTP test suite which simulates an OLTP application.

Ping

Don't underestimate the humble **ping** tool; along with being able to diagnose many network problems, it's round trip time is a handy guide as to the latency of a network link.

iPerf

iPerf allows you to conduct a series of network tests to determine the bandwidth between two servers.

Network benchmarking

There are a number of areas that we need to benchmark on the network to be able to understand any limitation and make sure there are no miss configurations.

A standard ethernet frame is 1500 bytes, a **jumbo frame** is typically 9000 bytes. This increased frame size reduces the overheads for sending data. If you have configured your network with a jumbo frame, the first thing to check is that they are configured correctly across all your servers and networking devices. If jumbo frames are configured incorrectly, Ceph will exhibit strange random behavior that is very hard to trace; therefore, it is essential that jumbo frames are configured correctly and confirmed to be working before deploying Ceph over the top of your network.

To confirm whether jumbo frames are working correctly, you can use `ping` to send large packets with the **don't fragment** flag set:

```
ping -M do -s 8972 <destination IP>
```

This command should be run across all your nodes to make sure they can ping each other using jumbo frames. If it fails, investigate the issue and resolve before deploying Ceph. It is also worth trying to automate this test, as future network changes could break this behavior, and diagnosing misconfigured jumbo frames through Ceph is almost impossible.

The next testing to undertake is to measure the round trip time also with the ping tool. Using the packet size parameter again but with the don't fragment flag, it is possible to test the round trip time of certain packet sizes up to 64 KB, which is the maximum IP packet size.

Here are some example readings between two hosts on a **10GBase-T** network:

- 32 B = 85 microseconds
- 4 KB = 112 microseconds
- 16 KB = 158 microseconds
- 64 KB = 248 microseconds

As you can see, larger packet sizes impact the round trip time; this is one reason why larger I/O sizes will see a decrease in IOPS in Ceph.

Finally, let's test the bandwidth between two hosts to confirm whether we get the expected performance or not.

Run `iperf -s` on the server that will run the iPerf server role:

```
------------------------------------------------------------
Server listening on TCP port 5001
TCP window size: 85.3 KByte (default)
------------------------------------------------------------
```

Then, run `iperf -c <address of iperf server>`:

```
------------------------------------------------------------
Client connecting to 10.1.111.1, TCP port 5001
TCP window size:  325 KByte (default)
------------------------------------------------------------
[  3] local 10.1.111.5 port 59172 connected with 10.1.111.1 port 5001
[ ID] Interval        Transfer      Bandwidth
[  3]  0.0-10.0 sec  11.1 GBytes  9.51 Gbits/sec
```

We can see that in this example, the two hosts are connected via a 10G network and obtain near the maximum theoretical throughput. If you do not see the correct throughput, then an investigation into the network, including host configuration, needs to be done.

Disk benchmarking

It is a good idea to understand the underlying performance of the hard disks and SSDs in your Ceph cluster, as this will enable you to predict the overall performance of your Ceph cluster. To benchmark the disks in your cluster, the fio tool will be used.

Use fio carefully if operating in write mode. If you specify a block device, fio will happily write over any data that exists on that disk

Fio is a complex tool with many configuration options. For the purpose of this chapter, we will concentrate on using it to perform basic read and write benchmarks:

1. Install the fio tool on a Ceph OSD node:

   ```
   apt-get install fio
   ```

   The preceding command gives the following output:

```
The following NEW packages will be installed
   fio
0 to upgrade, 1 to newly install, 0 to remove and 121 not to upgrade.
Need to get 368 kB of archives.
After this operation, 1,572 kB of additional disk space will be used.
Get:1 http://gb.archive.ubuntu.com/ubuntu xenial/universe amd64 fio amd64 2.2.10-1ubuntu1 [368 kB]
Fetched 368 kB in 5s (69.7 kB/s)
Selecting previously unselected package fio.
(Reading database ... 579847 files and directories currently installed.)
Preparing to unpack .../fio_2.2.10-1ubuntu1_amd64.deb ...
Unpacking fio (2.2.10-1ubuntu1) ...
Processing triggers for man-db (2.7.5-1) ...
Setting up fio (2.2.10-1ubuntu1) ...
```

2. Now, create a new file and place the following fio configuration into it:

   ```
   [global]
   ioengine=libaio
   randrepeat=0
   invalidate=0
   rw=randwrite
   bs=4k
   direct=1
   ```

```
time_based=1
runtime=30
numjobs=1
iodepth=1
filename=/test.fio
size=1G
```

The previous fio config will run a single threaded 4 KB random write test for 30 seconds. It will create a 1G `test.fio` file in the root of the filesystem. If you wish to target a block device directly, simply set the filename to the block device; but note that with the preceding warning, fio will overwrite any data on that block device.

Notice that the job is set to use direction, so the page cache will not accelerate any I/O operations.

To run the fio job, simply call `fio` with the name of the file to which you saved the previous config:

```
fio <filename>
```

The preceding command gives the following output:

```
file1: (g=0): rw=read, bs=4M-4M/4M-4M/4M-4M, ioengine=libaio, iodepth=1
fio-2.2.10
Starting 1 process
Jobs: 1 (f=1): [R(1)] [100.0% done] [100.0MB/0KB/0KB /s] [25/0/0 iops] [eta 00m:00s]
file1: (groupid=0, jobs=1): err= 0: pid=26999: Sun Mar 12 22:20:33 2017
  read : io=9496.0MB, bw=162052KB/s, iops=39, runt= 60005msec
    slat (usec): min=174, max=31852, avg=244.48, stdev=649.33
    clat (msec): min=15, max=338, avg=25.03, stdev=12.58
     lat (msec): min=15, max=338, avg=25.27, stdev=12.61
    clat percentiles (msec):
     |  1.00th=[    22],  5.00th=[    22], 10.00th=[    22], 20.00th=[    23],
     | 30.00th=[    23], 40.00th=[    23], 50.00th=[    24], 60.00th=[    24],
     | 70.00th=[    24], 80.00th=[    24], 90.00th=[    25], 95.00th=[    26],
     | 99.00th=[    80], 99.50th=[   102], 99.90th=[   182], 99.95th=[   223],
     | 99.99th=[   338]
    bw (KB  /s): min=77722, max=183641, per=100.00%, avg=163013.63, stdev=21774.82
    lat (msec) : 20=0.25%, 50=97.60%, 100=1.64%, 250=0.46%, 500=0.04%
  cpu          : usr=0.04%, sys=0.97%, ctx=2382, majf=0, minf=1036
  IO depths    : 1=100.0%, 2=0.0%, 4=0.0%, 8=0.0%, 16=0.0%, 32=0.0%, >=64=0.0%
     submit    : 0=0.0%, 4=100.0%, 8=0.0%, 16=0.0%, 32=0.0%, 64=0.0%, >=64=0.0%
     complete  : 0=0.0%, 4=100.0%, 8=0.0%, 16=0.0%, 32=0.0%, 64=0.0%, >=64=0.0%
     issued    : total=r=2374/w=0/d=0, short=r=0/w=0/d=0, drop=r=0/w=0/d=0
     latency   : target=0, window=0, percentile=100.00%, depth=1

Run status group 0 (all jobs):
   READ: io=9496.0MB, aggrb=162051KB/s, minb=162051KB/s, maxb=162051KB/s, mint=60005msec, maxt=60005msec
```

Once the job is done, fio will produce an output similar to the previous screenshot. You can see that the fio job runs 39 IOPS and 162 MBps on an average, and the average latency was 25 milliseconds.

There is also a breakdown of latency percentiles, which can be useful for understanding the spread of the request latency.

RADOS benchmarking

The next step is to benchmark the RADOS layer. This will give you a combined figure, including the performance of the disks, networking along with the overheads of the Ceph code, and extra replicated copies of data.

The RADOS command-line tool has a built-in benchmarking command, which by default initiates 16 threads, all writing 4 MB objects. To run the RADOS benchmark, run the following command:

```
rados -p rbd bench 10 write
```

This will run the write benchmark for 10 seconds:

```
Maintaining 16 concurrent writes of 4194304 bytes to objects of size 4194304 for up to 10 seconds or 0 objects
Object prefix: benchmark_data_ms-r1-c1-osd1_25645
  sec Cur ops   started  finished  avg MB/s  cur MB/s last lat(s)  avg lat(s)
    0      0         0         0         0         0          -           0
    1     16       121       105   419.977       420  0.0683843    0.138681
    2     15       254       239   477.947       536   0.139127    0.128909
    3     16       370       354   471.939       460  0.0906016    0.131449
    4     16       491       475   474.937       484  0.0822003    0.132115
    5     16       611       595   475.935       480   0.142927    0.132402
    6     16       731       715   476.602       480   0.110139    0.131169
    7     16       859       843    481.65       512  0.0932729    0.131419
    8     15       984       969   484.435       504   0.214752    0.131099
    9     16      1115      1099    488.38       520   0.131412    0.129911
   10     15      1229      1214   485.536       460    0.13085    0.130238
Total time run:         10.120543
Total writes made:      1230
Write size:             4194304
Object size:            4194304
Bandwidth (MB/sec):     486.14
Stddev Bandwidth:       34.0562
Max bandwidth (MB/sec): 536
Min bandwidth (MB/sec): 420
Average IOPS:           121
Stddev IOPS:            8
Max IOPS:               134
Min IOPS:               105
Average Latency(s):     0.13146
Stddev Latency(s):      0.0673788
Max latency(s):         0.703673
Min latency(s):         0.0400385
Cleaning up (deleting benchmark objects)
Clean up completed and total clean up time :0.701427
```

In the previous example, it can be seen that the cluster was able to sustain a write bandwidth of around 480 MBps. The output also gives you latency and other useful figures. Notice that at the end of the test, it deletes the objects created as part of the benchmark automatically. If you wish to use the RADOS tool to carry out read benchmarks, then you need to specify the `--no-cleanup` option to leave the objects in place, and then run the benchmark again with the benchmark type specified as `seq` instead of `write`. You will then manually need to clear the bench objects afterward.

RBD benchmarking

Finally, we will test the performance of RBDs using our favorite tool fio again. This will test the entire software and hardware stack, and the results will be very close to what clients would expect to observe. By configuring fio to emulate certain client applications, we can also get a feel for the expected performance of these applications.

To test the performance of an RBD, we will use the fio RBD engine, which allows fio to talk directly to the RBD image. Create a new fio config and place the following into it:

```
[global]
ioengine=rbd
randrepeat=0
clientname=admin
pool=rbd
rbdname=test
invalidate=0
rw=write
bs=1M
direct=1
time_based=1
runtime=30
numjobs=1
iodepth=1
```

You can see that, unlike the disk benchmarking configuration, instead of using the `libaio` engine, this config file now uses the `rbd` engine. When using the `rbd` engine, you also need to specify the RADOS pool and the `cephx` user. Finally, instead of specifying a filename or block device, you simply need to specify an RBD image that exists in the RADOS pool that you configured.

Then, run the fio job to test the performance of your RBDL:

```
Starting 1 process
rbd engine: RBD version: 0.1.10
Jobs: 1 (f=1): [W(1)] [100.0% done] [0KB/69632KB/0KB /s] [0/68/0 iops] [eta 00m:00s]
rbd_iodepth32: (groupid=0, jobs=1): err= 0: pid=5021: Sun Mar 12 22:29:13 2017
  write: io=2020.0MB, bw=68947KB/s, iops=67, runt= 30001msec
    slat (usec): min=11, max=1741, avg=36.49, stdev=39.93
    clat (msec): min=4, max=612, avg=14.81, stdev=37.84
     lat (msec): min=4, max=612, avg=14.85, stdev=37.84
    clat percentiles (msec):
     |  1.00th=[    5],  5.00th=[    5], 10.00th=[    5], 20.00th=[    5],
     | 30.00th=[    5], 40.00th=[    5], 50.00th=[    5], 60.00th=[    6],
     | 70.00th=[    6], 80.00th=[    9], 90.00th=[   30], 95.00th=[   60],
     | 99.00th=[  186], 99.50th=[  265], 99.90th=[  420], 99.95th=[  437],
     | 99.99th=[  611]
    bw (KB  /s): min= 7231, max=174080, per=100.00%, avg=71772.68, stdev=35752.42
    lat (msec) : 10=82.13%, 20=4.95%, 50=6.73%, 100=3.66%, 250=1.93%
    lat (msec) : 500=0.54%, 750=0.05%
  cpu          : usr=0.29%, sys=0.01%, ctx=2026, majf=0, minf=0
  IO depths    : 1=100.0%, 2=0.0%, 4=0.0%, 8=0.0%, 16=0.0%, 32=0.0%, >=64=0.0%
     submit    : 0=0.0%, 4=100.0%, 8=0.0%, 16=0.0%, 32=0.0%, 64=0.0%, >=64=0.0%
     complete  : 0=0.0%, 4=100.0%, 8=0.0%, 16=0.0%, 32=0.0%, 64=0.0%, >=64=0.0%
     issued    : total=r=0/w=2020/d=0, short=r=0/w=0/d=0, drop=r=0/w=0/d=0
     latency   : target=0, window=0, percentile=100.00%, depth=1

Run status group 0 (all jobs):
  WRITE: io=2020.0MB, aggrb=68947KB/s, minb=68947KB/s, maxb=68947KB/s, mint=30001msec, maxt=30001msec
```

Recommended tunings

Tuning your Ceph cluster will enable you to get the best performance and to get the most benefit from your hardware. In this section we will look at recommended Ceph tuning options.

CPU

As Ceph is software-defined for storage, its performance is heavily effected by the speed of the CPUs in the OSD nodes. Faster CPUs mean that the Ceph code can run faster and will spend less time processing each I/O request. The result is a lower latency per I/O, which, if the underlying storage can cope, will reduce the CPU as a bottleneck and give a higher overall performance. In Chapter 1, *Planning for Ceph*, it was advised that high Ghz processors should be preferred for performance reasons; however, there are additional concerns with high core count CPUs when they are over specified for the job.

To understand, we will need to cover a brief history on CPU design. During the early 2000s, CPUs were all single core designs, which ran constantly at the same frequency and didn't support many low power modes. As they moved to higher frequencies and core counts started, it became apparent that not every core would be able to run at its maximum frequency all the time. The amount of heat generated from the CPU package was simply too great. Fast forward to today, and this still holds true, there is no such thing as a 4 GHz 20 core CPU; it would simply generate too much heat to be feasible.

However, the clever people who designed CPUs came up with a solution, which allowed each core to run at a different frequency and also allowed them to power themselves down into deep sleep states. Both approaches lowered the power and cooling requirements of the CPU down to single figure watts. The CPUs have much lower clock speeds, but with the ability for a certain total number of cores to engage turbo mode, higher GHz are possible. There is normally a gradual decrease in the top turbo frequency as the number of active cores increases to keep the heat output below a certain threshold. If a low-threaded process is started, the CPU wakes up a couple of cores and speeds them up to a much higher frequency to get better single-threaded performance. In Intel CPUs, the different frequency levels are called **P-states** and sleep levels are called **C-states**.

This all sounds like the perfect package: a CPU that when idle consumes hardly any power, and yet when needed, it can turbo boost a handful of cores to achieve high clock speed. Unfortunately, as with most things in life, there is no such thing as a free lunch. There are some overheads with this approach that have a detrimental effect on the latency sensitive applications, with Ceph being one of them.

There are two main problems with this approach that impact the latency sensitive applications. The first being that it takes time for a core to wake up from a sleep state. The deeper the sleep, the longer it takes to wake up. The core has to reinitialize certain things before it is ready to be used. Here is a list from an Intel E3-1200v5 CPU; older CPUs may fair slightly worse:

- POLL = 0 microsecond
- C1-SKL = 2 microseconds
- C1E-SKL = 10 microseconds
- C3-SKL = 70 microseconds
- C6-SKL = 85 microseconds
- C7s-SKL = 124 microseconds
- C8-SKL = 200 microseconds

We can see that in a worse case, it may take a core up to 200 microseconds to wake up from its deepest sleep. When you consider that a single Ceph I/O may require several threads across several nodes to wake up a CPU core, these exit latencies can start to really add up. While P-states that effect the core frequency don't impact performance quite as much as the C-state exit latencies, the core's frequency doesn't immediately increase in a speed to maximum as soon as its in use. This means that under a low utilization, the CPU cores may only be operating at a low GHz. This leads onto the second problem that lies with the Linux scheduler.

Linux is aware of what core is active and which C-state and P-state each core is running at. It can fully control each core's behavior. Unfortunately, Linux's scheduler doesn't take any of this information into account, and instead, it prefers to try and balance threads across cores evenly. What this means is that with at low utilization, all the CPU cores will spend the bulk on their time in their lowest C-state and will operate at a low frequency. During a low utilization, this can impact the latency for small I/Os by 4-5x, which is a significant impact.

Until Linux has a power aware scheduler that will take into account which cores are already active and schedules threads on them to reduce latency, the best approach is to force the CPU to only sleep down to a certain C-state and also force it to run at the highest frequency all the time. This does increase the power draw, but in the newest models of CPU, this has somewhat been reduced. For this reason, it should be clear why it is recommended to size your CPU to your workload. Running a 40 core server at a high C-state and high frequency will consume a lot of power.

To force Linux to only drop down to the C1 C-state, add this to your GRUB config:

```
intel_idle.max_cstate=1
```

Some Linux distributions have a performance mode where this runs the CPUs at a maximum frequency. However, the manual way to achieve this is to echo values via sysfs. Sticking the following in the /etc/rc.local will set all your cores to run at their maximum frequency on the boot:

```
/sys/devices/system/cpu/intel_pstate/min_perf_pct
```

After you restart your OSD node, these changes should be in effect. Confirm by running these commands:

```
sudo cpupower monitor
```

As mentioned earlier in the chapter, before making the changes, run a reference benchmark, and then do it again afterwards so that you can understand the gains made by this change.

Filestore

Below are the items you can tune to improve the performance of Filestore.

VFS cache pressure

As the name suggests, the filestore object store works by storing RADOS objects as files on a standard Linux file system. In most cases, this will be XFS. As each object is stored as a file, there will likely be hundreds of thousands, if not millions, of files per disk. A Ceph cluster is comprised of 8 TB disks and is used for a RBD workload. Assuming the RBD is made up of the standard 4 MB objects, there would be nearly 2 million objects per disk.

When an application asks Linux to read or write to a file on a file system, it needs to know where that file actually exists on the disk. In order to find this location out, it needs to follow the structure of directory entries and inodes. Each one of these look ups will require disk access if it's not already cached in memory. This can lead to poor performance in some cases if the Ceph objects, which are required to be read or written to, haven't been accessed in a while and are hence not cached. This penalty is a lot higher in spinning disk clusters as opposed to SSD-based clusters due to the impact of the random reads.

By default, Linux favors the caching of data in the pagecache versus the caching of inodes and directory entries. In many cases in Ceph, this is the opposite of what you actually want to happen. Luckily, there is a tuneable kernel that allows you to tell Linux to prefer directory entries and inodes over pagecache; this can be controlled by the following sysctl setting:

```
vm.vfs_cache_pressure
```

Where a lower number sets a preference to cache inodes and directory entries, do not set this to zero. A zero setting tells the kernel not to flush old entries even in the event of a low memory condition and can have adverse effects. A value of 1 is recommended.

WBThrottle and/or nr_requests

Filestore uses buffered I/O to write; this brings a number of advantages if the filestore journal is on a faster media. Client requests are acknowledged as soon as they are written to the journal, and are then flushed to the data disk at a later date by the standard writeback functionality in Linux. This allows the spinning disk OSDs to provide write latency similar to SSDs when writing in small bursts. The delayed writeback also allows the kernel to rearrange I/O requests to the disk to hopefully either coalesce them, or allow the disk heads to take a more optimal path across the platters. The end effect is that you can squeeze some more I/O out of each disk than what would be possible with a direct or sync I/O.

However, the problem occurs when the amount of incoming writes to the Ceph cluster outstrips the capabilities of the underlying disks. In this scenario, the number of pending I/Os waiting to be written on disk can increase uncontrollably, and the resulting queue of I/Os can saturate the disk and Ceph queues. Read requests are particularly badly effected, as they get stuck behind potentially thousands of write requests, which may take several seconds to flush to the disk.

In order to combat this problem, Ceph has a writeback throttle mechanism built into filestore called **WBThrottle**. It is designed to limit the amount of writeback I/Os that can queue up and start the flushing process earlier than what would be naturally triggered by the kernel. Unfortunately, testing has shown that the defaults may still not curtail the behavior that can reduce the impact on the read latency. Tuning can alter this behavior to reduce the write queue lengths and allow reads not to get effected much. However, there is a trade-off; by reducing the maximum number of writes allowed to be queued up, you can reduce the kernel's opportunity to maximize the efficiency of reordering the requests. Some thought needs to be given to what is important for your given use case, workloads, and tune to match it.

To control the writeback queue depth, you can either reduce the maximum amount of outstanding I/Os using Ceph's WBThrottle settings, or lower the maximum outstanding requests at the block layer in the kernel. Both can effectively control the same behavior, and it's really a preference on how you prefer to implement the configuration.

It should also be noted that the operation priorities in Ceph are more effective with a shorter queue at the disk level. By shortening the queue at the disk, the main queueing location moves up into Ceph where it has more control over what I/O has priority. Consider the following example:

```
echo 8 > /sys/block/sda/queue/nr_requests
```

With the release of the Linux 4.10 kernel, a new feature was introduced which deprioritizes writeback I/O; this greatly reduces the impact of write starvation with Ceph and is worth investigating if running the 4.10 kernel is feasible.

Filestore queue throttling

In the default configuration, when a disk becomes saturated, its disk queue will gradually fill up. Then, the filestore queue will start to fill up. Up until this point, I/O would have been accepted as fast as the journal could accept it. As soon as the filestore queue fills up and/or the WBThrottle kicks in, I/O will suddenly be stopped until the queues fall back below the thresholds. This behavior will lead to large spikes and, most likely, periods of low performance, where other client requests will experience high latency.

In order to reduce the spikiness of filestore when the disks become saturated, there are some additonal configuration options that can be set to gradually throttle back operations as the filestore queue fills up, instead of bouncing around the hard limit.

filestore_queue_low_threshhold

This is expressed as a percentage between 0.0 and 1.0. Below this threshold, no throttling is performed.

filestore_queue_high_threshhold

This is expressed as a percentage between 0.0 and 1.0. Between the low and high threshold, throttling is carried out by introducing a per I/O delay, which is linearly increased from 0 to `filestore_queue_high_delay_multiple/filestore_expected_throughput_ops`.

And then from the high threshold to max, it will throttle at the rate determined by `filestore_queue_max_delay_multiple/filestore_expected_throughput_ops`

Both of these throttle rates use the configured one, which is expected throughout of the disk to calculate the correct delay to introduce. The `delay_multiple` variables are there to allow an increase of this delay if the queue goes over the high threshold.

filestore_expected_throughput_ops

This should be set to the expected IOPS performance of the underlying disk where the OSD is running.

filestore_queue_high_delay_multiple

Between the low and high thresholds, this multiple is used to calculate the correct amount of delay to introduce

filestore_queue_max_delay_multiple

Above the maximum queue size, this multiplier is used to calculate an even greater delay to hopefully stop the queue from ever filling up.

PG Splitting

A filesystem has a limit on the number of files that can be stored in a directory before performance starts to degrade when asked to list the contents. As Ceph storing millions of objects per disk, which are just files, it splits the files across a nested directory structure to limit the number of files placed in each directory. As the number of objects in the cluster increases, so does the number of files per directory. When the number of files in these directories exceed these limits, Ceph splits the directory into further sub directories and migrates the objects to them. This operation can have a significant performance penalty when it occurs. Furthermore, XFS tries to place its files in the same directory close together on the disk. When PG splitting occurs, fragmentation of the XFS filesystem can occur, leading to further performance degradation.

By default, Ceph will split a PG when it contains 320 objects. An 8 TB disk in a Ceph cluster configured with the recommended number of PGs per OSD will likely have over 5000 objects per PG. This PG would have gone through several PG split operations in its lifetime, resulting in a deeper and more complex directory structure.

As mentioned previously in the VFS cache pressure section, to avoid costly dentry lookups, the kernel tries to cache them. The result of PG splitting means that there is a higher number of directories to cache, and there may not be enough memory to cache them all, leading to poorer performance.

A common approach to this problem is to increase the allowed number of files in each directory by setting the OSD configuration options as follows:

```
filestore_split_multiple
```

also this setting

```
filestore_merge_threshold
```

With the formula here, you can set at what threshold Ceph will split a PG:

filestore_split_multiple * abs(filestore_merge_threshold)*16

Care should be taken. Although increasing the threshold will reduce the occurences of PG splitting and also reduce the complexity of the directory structure, when a PG split does occur, it will have to split far more objects. The greater the number of objects that will need to be split will have a bigger impact on performance and may even lead to OSD's timing out. There is a trade-off of split frequency to split time; the defaults may be slightly on the conservative side, especially with larger disks.

Doubling or tripling the split threshold can probably be done safely without too much concern; greater values should be tested with the cluster under I/O load before putting it into production.

Scrubbing

Scrubbing is Ceph's way of verifying that the objects stored in RADOS are consistent, and to protect against bit rot or other corruptions. Scrubbing can either be normal or deep, depending on the set schedule. During a normal scrub operation, Ceph reads all objects for a certain PG and compares the copies to make sure that their size and attributes match. A deep scrub operation goes one step further and compares the actual data contents of the objects. This generates a lot more I/O than the simpler standard scrubbing routine. Normal scrubbing is carried out daily, whereas deep scrubbing is attempted to be carried out weekly due to the extra I/O load.

Despite being deprioritized, scrubbing does have an impact on client IO, and so, there are a number of OSD settings that can be tweaked to guide Ceph as to when it should carry out the scrubbing.

The osd _scrub_begin_hour and osd _scrub_end_hour OSD configuration options determine the window Ceph will try and schedule scrubs in. By default, these are set to allow scrubbing to occur throughout the 24-hour period. If your workload only runs through the day, you might want to adjust the scrub start and end times to tell Ceph that you want it to scrub during off peak times only.

It should be noted that this time, a window is only honored if the PG has not fallen outside its maximum scrub interval. If it has, then it will be scrubbed regardless of the time window settings. The default max intervals for both normal and deep scrubs are set to one week.

OP priorities

Ceph has the ability to prioritize certain operations over others, with the idea that the client I/Os should have precedence over the recovery, scrubbing, and snapshot trimming IO. These priorities are controlled by the following configuration options:

```
osd client op priority
osd recovery op priority
osd scrub priority
osd snap trim priority
```

Here, the higher the value, the higher priority. The default values work fairly well, and there shouldn't be much requirement to change them. But there can be some benefit in lowering the priority of scrub and recovery operations to limit their impact on the client I/O. It's important to understand that Ceph can only prioritize the I/O in the sections of the I/O path that it controls. Therefore, tuning the disk queue lengths in the previous section may be needed to get maximum benefit.

The Network

The network is a core component of a Ceph cluster, and its performance will greatly affect the overall performance of the cluster. 10 GB should be treated as a minimum; 1 GB networking will not provide the required latency for a high performance Ceph cluster. There are a number of tunings that can help to improve the network performance by decreasing latency and increasing throughput.

The first thing to consider if you wish to use jumbo frames is using an MTU of 9000 instead of 1500; each I/O request can be sent using less Ethernet frames. As each Ethernet frame has a small overhead, increasing the maximum Ethernet frame to 9000 can help. In practice, gains are normally less than 5% and should be weighed up against the disadvantages of having to make sure every device is configured correctly.

The following network options set in your `sysctl.conf` are recommended to maximize network performance:

```
#Network buffers
net.core.rmem_max = 56623104
net.core.wmem_max = 56623104
```

```
net.core.rmem_default = 56623104
net.core.wmem_default = 56623104
net.core.optmem_max = 40960
net.ipv4.tcp_rmem = 4096 87380 56623104
net.ipv4.tcp_wmem = 4096 65536 56623104

#Maximum connections and backlog
net.core.somaxconn = 1024
net.core.netdev_max_backlog = 50000

#TCP tuning options
net.ipv4.tcp_max_syn_backlog = 30000
net.ipv4.tcp_max_tw_buckets = 2000000
net.ipv4.tcp_tw_reuse = 1
net.ipv4.tcp_tw_recycle = 1
net.ipv4.tcp_fin_timeout = 10

#Don't use slow start on idle TCP connections
net.ipv4.tcp_slow_start_after_idle = 0
```

 If you are using ipv6 for your Ceph cluster, make sure you use the appropriate ipv6 sysctl options.

General system tuning

There are a number of general system parameters that are recommended to be tuned to best suit Ceph's performance requirements. The settings below can be added to your `/etc/sysctl.conf` file.

#Make sure that the system has sufficient memory free at all times:

```
vm/min_free_kbytes = 524288
```

Increase the maximum number of allowed processes:

```
kernel.pid_max=4194303
```

#Maximum number of file handles:

```
fs.file-max=26234859
```

Kernel RBD

The Linux kernel RBD driver allows you to directly map Ceph RBDs as standard Linux block devices and use them in the same way as any other device. Generally, kernel mapped RBDs need minimum configuration, but in some special cases some tuning maybe necessary.

Firstly, it is recommended to use a kernel that is as new as possible because newer kernels will have better RBD support, and in some cases, improved performance.

Queue Depth

Since kernel 4.0, the RBD driver uses `blk-mq`, which is designed to offer higher performance than the older queuing system. By default, the maximum outstanding requests possible with RBD when using `blk-mq` is 128. For most use cases, this is more than enough; however, if your workload needs to utilize the full power of a large Ceph cluster, then you may find that only having 128 outstanding requests is not enough. There is an option that can be specified when mapping the RBD to increase this value and can be set next.

ReadAhead

By default, RBD will be configured with a 128 KB readahead. If your workload mainly involves large sequential reading, then you can get a significant boost in performance by increasing the readahead value. In kernels before 4.4, there was a limitation where readahead values bigger than 2 MB were ignored. In most storage systems, this was not an issue, as the stripe sizes would have been smaller than 2 MB. As long as readahead is bigger than the stripe size, all the disks will be involved and performance will increase.

By default, a Ceph RBD is striped across 4 MB objects, and so, an RBD has a chunk size of 4 MB and a stripe size = 4 MB*Number of OSDS in the cluster. Therefore, with a readahead size smaller than 4 MB, most of the time readahead will be doing very little to improve performance, and you will likely see that read's performance is struggling to exceed that of a single OSD.

In kernel 4.4 and above, you can set the readahead value much higher and experience read performance in the hundreds of MBs in a second range.

PG distributions

While not strictly a performance tuning option, ensuring even PG distribution across your Ceph cluster is an essential task that should be undertaken during the early stages of the deployment of your cluster. As Ceph uses CRUSH to pseudo randomly determine where to place data, it will not always balance PG equally across every OSD. A Ceph cluster that is not balanced will be unable to take full advantage of the raw capacity, as the most oversubscribed OSD will effectively become the limit to the capacity.

An unevenly balanced cluster will mean that a higher number of requests will be targeted at the OSDs holding the most PGs. These OSDS will then place an artificial performance ceiling on the cluster, especially if the cluster is comprised of spinning disk OSDS.

To rebalance PGs across a Ceph cluster, you simply have to reweight the OSD so that CRUSH adjusts how many PGs will be stored on it. It's important to note that, by default, the weight of every OSD is 1, and you cannot weight an underutilized OSD above 1 to increase its utilization. The only option is to decrease the reweight value of over-utilized OSDs, which should move PGs to the less utilized OSDS.

It is also important to understand that there is a difference between the CRUSH weight of an OSD and the reweight value. The reweight value is used as an override to correct the misplacement from the CRUSH algorithm. The reweight command only effects the OSD and will not affect the weight of the bucket (for example, host), that it is a member of. It is also reset to 1.0 on restart of the OSD. While this can be frustrating, it's important to understand that any future modification to the cluster, be it increasing the number of PGs or adding additional OSDs, would have likely made any reweight value incorrect. Therefore, reweighting OSDs should not be looked at as a one-time operation, but something that is being continuously done and will adjust to the changes in the cluster.

To reweight an OSD, simply use this simple command:

```
Ceph osd reweight <osd number> <weight value 0.0-1.0>
```

Once executed, Ceph will start backfilling to move PGs to their newly assigned OSDS.

Of course, searching through all your OSDS and trying to find the OSD that needs weighting, and then running this command for everyone, would be a very lengthy process. Luckily, there is another Ceph tool that can automate a large part of this process:

```
ceph osd reweight-by-utilisation <threshold> <max change>
<number of OSDs>
```

This command will compare all the OSDs in your cluster and change the override weighting of the top *N* most OSDs, where *N* is controlled by the last parameter, which is over the threshold value. You can also limit the maximum change applied to each OSD by specifying the second parameter: 0.05 or 5% is normally a recommended figure.

There is also a `test-reweight-by-utilization` command, which will allow you to see what the command would do before running it.

While this command is safe to use, there are a number of things that should be taken into consideration before running it:

- It has no concept of different pools on different OSDs. If, for example, you have an SSD tier and an HDD tier, the `reweight-by-utilization` command will still try and balance data across all OSDs. If your SSD tier is not as full as the HDD tier, the command will not work as expected. If you wish to balance OSDs confined to a single bucket, look into the script version of this command created by Cern.
- It is possible to reweight the cluster to the point that CRUSH is unable to determine placement for some PGs. If recovery halts and one or more PGs are left in a remapped state, then this is likely what has happened. Simply increase or reset the reweight values to fix it.

Once you are confident with the operation of the command, it is possible to schedule it via `cron` so that your cluster is kept in a more balanced state automatically.

Summary

You should now have extensive knowledge on how to tune a Ceph cluster to maximize performance and achieve lower latency. Through the use of benchmarks, you should now be able to perform before and after tests to confirm if your tunings have had the desired effect. It is worth reviewing the official Ceph documentation to get a better understanding of some of the other configuration options that may be beneficial to your cluster.

10
Troubleshooting

Ceph is largely autonomous in taking care of itself and recovering from failure scenarios, but in some cases human intervention is required. This chapter will look at such common errors and failure scenarios and how to bring Ceph back to working by troubleshooting them. You will learn the following topics:

- How to correctly repair inconsistent objects
- How to solve problems with the help of peering
- How to deal with `near_full` and `too_full` OSDs
- How to investigate errors via Ceph logging
- How to investigate poor performance
- How to investigate PGs in a down state

Repairing inconsistent objects

We will now see how we can correctly repair inconsistent objects.

1. To be able to recreate an inconsistent scenario, create an RBD, and later we'll make a file system on it:

```
vagrant@mon1:~$ sudo rbd create test --size=1G
vagrant@mon1:~$ sudo rbd feature disable test exclusive-lock object-map fast-diff deep-flatten
vagrant@mon1:~$ sudo rbd map test
/dev/rbd0
vagrant@mon1:~$ sudo mkfs.ext4 /dev/rbd0
mke2fs 1.42.13 (17-May-2015)
Discarding device blocks: done
Creating filesystem with 262144 4k blocks and 65536 inodes
Filesystem UUID: a95d7f60-3be3-4c15-bafd-9d37559174db
Superblock backups stored on blocks:
        32768, 98304, 163840, 229376

Allocating group tables: done
Writing inode tables: done
Creating journal (8192 blocks): done
Writing superblocks and filesystem accounting information: done
```

2. Now, check to see which objects have been created by formatting the RBD with a file system:

```
root@mon1:/home/vagrant# rados -p rbd ls
rbd_data.1e502238e1f29.0000000000000086
rbd_data.1e502238e1f29.0000000000000000
rbd_data.1e502238e1f29.0000000000000083
rbd_data.1e502238e1f29.0000000000000060
rbd_data.1e502238e1f29.0000000000000004
```

3. Pick one object at random and use the `osd map` command to find out which PG the object is stored in:

```
root@mon1:/home/vagrant# ceph osd map rbd rbd_data.1e502238e1f29.0000000000000086
osdmap e234 pool 'rbd' (0) object 'rbd_data.1e502238e1f29.0000000000000086' -> pg 0.5ee4eb42 (0.2)
> up ([1,0,2], p1) acting_([1,0,2], p1)
```

4. Find this object on the disk on one of the OSD nodes; in this case, it is `OSD.0` on `OSD1`:

```
vagrant@osd1:~$ sudo ls -l /var/lib/ceph/osd/ceph-0/current/0.5_head/
total 4096
-rw-r--r--  1 ceph ceph        0 Feb  7 22:07 __head_00000005__0
-rw-r--r--  1 ceph ceph 4194304 Mar 17 21:28 rbd\udata.1e502238e1f29.0000000000000083__head_327C8305__0
```

5. Corrupt it by echoing garbage over the top of it:

```
root@osd1:/home/vagrant# echo blah > /var/lib/ceph/osd/ceph-0/current/0.5_head/rbd\udata.1e502238e1f29.
0000000000000083__head_327C8305__0
```

6. Now, tell Ceph to do a scrub on the PG that contains the object that we corrupted:

```
root@mon1:/home/vagrant# ceph pg deep-scrub 0.5
instructing pg 0.5 on osd.2 to deep-scrub
```

7. If you check the Ceph status, you will see that Ceph has detected the corrupted object and marked the PG as inconsistent. From this point onward, forget that we corrupted the object manually and work through the process as if it were for real:

```
root@mon1:/home/vagrant# ceph -s
    cluster d9f58afd-3e62-4493-ba80-0356290b3d9f
     health HEALTH_ERR
            1 pgs inconsistent
            3 scrub errors
            too many PGs per OSD (320 > max 300)
            all OSDs are running kraken or later but the 'require_kraken_osds' osdmap flag is not set
     monmap e2: 3 mons at {mon1=192.168.0.41:6789/0,mon2=192.168.0.42:6789/0,mon3=192.168.0.43:6789/0}
            election epoch 158, quorum 0,1,2 mon1,mon2,mon3
        mgr active: mon2 standbys: mon3, mon1
     osdmap e234: 3 osds: 3 up, 3 in
            flags sortbitwise,require_jewel_osds
      pgmap v3879: 320 pgs, 4 pools, 37575 kB data, 23 objects
            229 MB used, 26665 MB / 26894 MB avail
                 319 active+clean
                   1 active+clean+inconsistent
```

By looking at the detailed health report, we can find the PG that contains the corrupted object. We could just tell Ceph to repair the PG now; however, if the primary OSD is the one that holds the corrupted object, it will overwrite the remaining good copies. This would be bad; thus in order to make sure this doesn't happen, before running the repair command we will confirm which OSD holds the corrupt object.

```
root@mon1:/home/vagrant# ceph health detail
HEALTH_ERR 1 pgs inconsistent; 3 scrub errors; too many PGs per OSD (320 > max 300); all OSDs are running kr
aken or later but the 'require_kraken_osds' osdmap flag is not set
pg 0.5 is active+clean+inconsistent, acting [2,0,1]
3 scrub errors
```

By looking at the health report we can see the three OSD's which hold a copy of the object; the first OSD is the primary.

8. Log onto the primary OSD node and open the log file for the primary OSD. You should be able to find the log entry where it indicates what object was flagged up by the PG scrub.

9. Now by logging on to each OSD and navigating through the PG structure, find the object mentioned in the log file and calculate a md5sum of each copy.

```
root@osd1:/var/lib/ceph/osd/ceph-0/current/0.5_head# md5sum rbd\\udata.1e502238e1f29.0000000000000083__head_327C8305__0
\0d599f0ec05c3bda8c3b8a68c32a1b47  rbd\\udata.1e502238e1f29.0000000000000083__head_327C8305__0
```

md5sum of object on osd node one

```
root@osd2:/home/vagrant# cd /var/lib/ceph/osd/ceph-2/current/0.5_head/
root@osd2:/var/lib/ceph/osd/ceph-2/current/0.5_head# md5sum rbd\\udata.1e502238e1f29.0000000000000083__
head_327C8305__0
\b5cfa9d6c8febd618f91ac2843d50a1c  rbd\\udata.1e502238e1f29.0000000000000083__head_327C8305__0
```

md5sum of object on osd node two

```
root@osd3:/home/vagrant# cd /var/lib/ceph/osd/ceph-1/current/0.5_head/
root@osd3:/var/lib/ceph/osd/ceph-1/current/0.5_head# md5sum rbd\\udata.1e502238e1f29.0000000000000083__
head_327C8305__0
\b5cfa9d6c8febd618f91ac2843d50a1c  rbd\\udata.1e502238e1f29.0000000000000083__head_327C8305__0
```

md5sum of object on osd node three.

We can see that the object on OSD.0 has a different md5sum, and so we know that it is the corrupt object.

```
OSD.0 = \0d599f0ec05c3bda8c3b8a68c32a1b47
OSD.2 = \b5cfa9d6c8febd618f91ac2843d50a1c
OSD.3 = \b5cfa9d6c8febd618f91ac2843d50a1c
```

Although we already know which copy of the object was corrupted as we manually corrupted the object on OSD.0, let's pretend we hadn't done it, and this corruption was caused by some random cosmic ray. We now have the md5sum of the three replica copies and can clearly see that the copy on OSD.0 is wrong. This is a big reason why a 2x replication scheme is bad; if a PG becomes inconsistent, you can't figure out which one is the bad one. As the primary OSD for this PG is 2, as can be seen in both the Ceph health details and the Ceph OSD map commands, we can safely run the ceph pg repair command without the fear of copying the bad object over the top of the remaining good copies.

```
root@mon1:/home/vagrant# ceph pg repair 0.5
instructing pg 0.5 on osd.2 to repair
```

We can see that the inconsistent PG has repaired itself:

```
root@mon1:/home/vagrant# ceph -s
    cluster d9f58afd-3e62-4493-ba80-0356290b3d9f
     health HEALTH_WARN
            too many PGs per OSD (320 > max 300)
            all OSDs are running kraken or later but the 'require_kraken_osds' osdmap flag is not
     monmap e2: 3 mons at {mon1=192.168.0.41:6789/0,mon2=192.168.0.42:6789/0,mon3=192.168.0.43:67
            election epoch 158, quorum 0,1,2 mon1,mon2,mon3
        mgr active: mon2 standbys: mon3, mon1
     osdmap e234: 3 osds: 3 up, 3 in
            flags sortbitwise,require_jewel_osds
      pgmap v3900: 320 pgs, 4 pools, 37575 kB data, 23 objects
            229 MB used, 26665 MB / 26894 MB avail
                 320 active+clean
```

In the event that the copy is corrupt on the primary OSD, then the following steps should be taken:

1. Stop the primary OSD.
2. Delete the object from the PG directory.
3. Restart the OSD.
4. Instruct Ceph to repair the PG.

Full OSDs

By default, Ceph will warn when OSD utilization approaches 85%, and it will stop write I/O to the OSD when it reaches 95%. If, for some reason, the OSD completely fills up to 100%, then the OSD is likely to crash and will refuse to come back online. An OSD that is above the 85% warning level will also refuse to participate in backfilling, so the recovery of the cluster may be impacted when OSDs are in a near full state.

Before covering the troubleshooting steps around full OSDs, it is highly recommended that you monitor the capacity utilization of your OSDs, as described in the monitoring chapter. This will give you advanced warning as OSDs approach the near_full warning threshold.

If you find yourself in a situation where your cluster is above the near full warning state, you have two main options:

1. Add some more OSDs.
2. Delete some data.

However, in the real world, both of these are either impossible or will take time, in which case the situation can deteriorate. If the OSD is only at the `near_full` threshold, then you can probably get things back on track by checking whether your OSD utilization is balanced, and then you can perform PG balancing if not. This was covered in more detail in the tuning chapter. The same applies to the `too_full` OSDs as well; although you are unlikely going to get them back below 85%, at least you can resume write operations.

If your OSDs have completely filled up, then they are in an offline state and will refuse to start. Now, you have an additional problem. If the OSDs will not start, then no matter what rebalancing or deletion of data you carry out, it will not be reflected on the full OSDs as they are offline. The only way to recover from this situation is to manually delete some PGs from the disk's file system to let the OSD start.

The following steps should be undertaken for this:

1. Make sure the OSD process is not running.
2. Set `nobackfill` on the cluster, to stop the recovery from happening when the OSD comes back online.
3. Find a PG that is in an active, clean, and remapped state and exists on the offline OSD.
4. Delete this PG from the offline OSD.
5. Hopefully you should now be able to restart the OSD.
6. Delete data from the Ceph cluster or rebalance PG's.
7. Remove nobackfill.
8. Run a scrub and repair the PG you just deleted.

Ceph logging

When investigating errors, it is very handy to be able to look through the Ceph log files to get a better idea of what is going on. By default, the logging levels are set so that only the important events are logged. During troubleshooting the logging levels may need to be increased in order to reveal the cause of the error. To increase the logging level, you can either edit `ceph.conf`, add the new logging level, and then restart the component, or, if you don't wish to restart the Ceph daemons, you can inject the new configuration parameter into the live running daemon. To inject parameters, use the ceph `tell` command:

```
ceph tell osd.0 injectargs --debug-osd 0/5
```

Then, set the logging level for the OSD log on `osd.0` to `0/5`. The number 0 is the disk logging level, and the number 5 is the in memory logging level.

 At a logging level of 20, the logs are extremely verbose and will grow quickly. Do not keep high verbosity logging enabled for too long. Higher logging levels will also have an impact on performance.

Slow performance

Slow performance is defined when the cluster is actively processing IO requests, but it appears to be operating at a lower performance level than what is expected. Generally, slow performance is caused by a component of your Ceph cluster reaching saturation and becoming a bottleneck. This maybe due to an increased number of client requests or a component failure that is causing Ceph to perform recovery.

Causes

Although there are many things which may cause Ceph to experience slow performance, here are some of the most likely causes.

Increased client workload

Sometimes, slow performance may not be due to an underlying fault; it may just be that the number and the type of client requests may have exceeded the capability of the hardware. Whether this is due to a number of separate workloads all running at the same time, or just a slow general increase over a period of time, if you are capturing the number of client requests across your cluster, this should be easy to trend. If the increased workload looks like it's permanent, then the only solution is to add some additional hardware.

Down OSDs

If a significant number of OSDs are marked down in a cluster, perhaps due to a whole OSD node going offline, although recovery will not start until the OSD's are marked out, the performance will be affected, as the number of IOPs available to service the client IO will now be lower. Your monitoring solution should alert you if this is happening and allow you to take action.

Recovery and backfilling

When an OSD is marked out, the affected PGs will re-peer with new OSDs and start the process of recovering and backfilling data across the cluster. This process can can put strain on the disks in a Ceph cluster and lead to higher latencies for client requests. There are several tuning options that can reduce the impact of backfilling by reducing the rate and priority. These should be evaluated against the impact of slower recovery from failed disks, which may reduce the durability of the cluster.

Scrubbing

When Ceph performs deep scrubbing to check your data for any inconsistencies, it has to read all the objects from the OSD; this can be a very IO-intensive task, and on large drives, the process can take a long time. Scrubbing is vital to protect against data loss and therefore should not be disabled. Various tuning options were discussed in `Chapter 9`, *Tuning Ceph* regarding setting windows for scrubbing and its priority. By tweaking these settings, a lot of the performance impact on client workloads from scrubbing can be avoided.

Snaptrimming

When you remove a snapshot, Ceph has to delete all the objects which have been created due to the copy on write nature of the snapshot process. From Ceph 10.2.8 onward, there is an improved OSD setting called `osd_snap_trim_sleep`, which makes Ceph wait for the specified number of settings between the trimming of each snapshot object. This ensures that the backing object store does not become overloaded.

> Although this setting was available in previous jewel releases, its behavior was not the same and should not be used.

Hardware or driver issues

If you have recently introduced new hardware into your Ceph cluster and, after backfilling has rebalanced your data, you start experiencing slow performance, check for firmware or driver updates relating to your hardware, as newer drivers may require a newer kernel. If you have only introduced a small amount of hardware, then you can temporarily mark the OSDs out on it without going below your pool's `min_size`; this can be a good way to rule out hardware issues.

Monitoring

This is where the monitoring you configured in Chapter 8, *Tiering with Ceph*, can really come in useful, as it will allow you to compare long-term trends with current metric readings and see if there are any clear anomalies.

It is recommended you first look at the disk performance as, in most cases of poor performance, the underlying disks are normally the components that become the bottleneck.

If you do not have monitoring configured or wish to manually drill deeper into the performance metrics, then there are a number of tools you can use to accomplish this.

iostat

iostat can be used to get a running overview of the performance and latency of all the disks running in your OSD nodes. Run iostat with the following command:

```
iostat -d 1 -x
```

You will get a display similar to this, which will refresh once a second:

Device:	rrqm/s	wrqm/s	r/s	w/s	rkB/s	wkB/s	avgrq-sz	avgqu-sz	await	r_await	w_await	svctm	%util
sda	0.00	4.00	2.00	24.00	68.00	9396.00	728.00	0.34	12.92	12.00	13.00	8.77	22.80
sdc	0.00	9.00	17.00	42.00	548.00	20468.00	712.41	1.11	18.71	27.76	15.05	10.17	60.00
sdd	0.00	8.00	9.00	51.00	36.00	20888.00	697.47	1.61	26.93	27.56	26.82	8.53	51.20
sdb	0.00	2.00	10.00	18.00	416.00	8108.00	608.86	0.43	15.29	16.00	14.89	5.57	15.60
nvme0n1	0.00	0.00	0.00	1254.00	0.00	126556.00	201.84	1.66	1.32	0.00	1.32	0.06	8.00
sde	0.00	2.00	10.00	9.00	416.00	3304.00	391.58	0.26	12.84	12.40	13.33	12.42	23.60
sdf	1.00	1.00	78.00	9.00	20492.00	3820.00	558.90	1.05	12.09	9.03	38.67	4.87	42.40
sdg	0.00	18.00	117.00	108.00	29600.00	47020.00	681.07	14.59	55.38	8.17	106.52	3.70	83.20
sdh	0.00	3.00	2.00	35.00	384.00	15816.00	875.68	0.38	10.38	10.00	10.40	5.41	20.00
sdi	0.00	1.00	83.00	15.00	20508.00	7024.00	561.88	1.56	15.96	7.57	62.40	3.59	35.20
sdj	0.00	5.00	87.00	52.00	14740.00	18760.00	482.01	2.78	25.84	11.77	49.38	7.19	100.00
sdk	0.00	0.00	3.00	160.00	12.00	5748.00	70.67	11.08	350.06	17.33	356.30	1.84	30.00
sdl	0.00	0.00	6.00	0.00	24.00	0.00	8.00	0.07	11.33	11.33	0.00	9.33	5.60

As a rule of thumb, if a large number of your disks are showing a high % util over a period of time, it is likely that your disks are being saturated. It may also be worth looking at the r_await time to see if read requests are taking longer than what should be expected for the type of disk in your OSD nodes. As mentioned earlier, if you find that high disk utilization is the cause of slow performance and the triggering factor is unlikely to dissipate soon, then extra disks are the only solution.

htop

Like the standard top utility, htop provides a live view of the CPU and the memory consumption of the host. However, it also produces a more intuitive display that may make judging overall system resource use easier, especially with the rapidly changing resource usage of Ceph.

```
  1  [||||                                        8.9%]    5  [|||||                                       9.5%]
  2  [|||||||||||||                              25.6%]    6  [||||                                        8.0%]
  3  [||||||||||                                 20.0%]    7  [||||||||                                   14.9%]
  4  [||||||||||                                 16.7%]    8  [||                                          4.4%]
  Mem[|||||||||||||||||||||||||||||||||||23.8G/62.7G]    Tasks: 49, 7845 thr; 1 running
  Swp[|                                      88.2M/9.31G]   Load average: 6.46 6.33 6.09
                                                           Uptime: 7 days, 08:32:23

    PID USER      PRI  NI  VIRT   RES   SHR S CPU% MEM%   TIME+  Command
   7308 ceph       20   0 2662M 1045M  6788 S 11.9  1.6 13h51:18 /usr/bin/ceph-osd -f --cluster ceph
   3945 ceph       20   0 2778M 1059M  7996 S 11.9  1.7 14h12:58 /usr/bin/ceph-osd -f --cluster ceph
```

atop

atop is another useful tool; it captures performance metrics for CPU, RAM, disk, network, and can present this all in one view; this makes it very easy to get a complete overview of the system resource usage.

Diagnostics

There are a number of internal Ceph tools that can be used to help diagnose a slow performance. The most useful command for investigating slow performance is dumping current in-flight operations, which can be done with a command such as the following:

```
sudo ceph daemon osd.x dump_ops_in_flight
```

This will dump all current operations for the specified OSD and break down all the various timings for each step of the operation. Here is an example of an inflight IO:

```
            "description": "osd_op(client.29342781.1:262455793 17.768b3a6 rb.0.4d983.238e1
f29.000000001988 [set-alloc-hint object_size 4194304 write_size 4194304,write 1318912~1228
8] snapc 0=[] ondisk+write e98614)",
            "initiated_at": "2017-04-21 22:23:11.401997",
            "age": 0.000626,
            "duration": 0.000704,
            "type_data": [
                "waiting for sub ops",
                {
                    "client": "client.29342781",
                    "tid": 262455793
                },
                [
                    {
                        "time": "2017-04-21 22:23:11.401997",
                        "event": "initiated"
                    },
                    {
                        "time": "2017-04-21 22:23:11.402107",
                        "event": "queued_for_pg"
                    },
                    {
                        "time": "2017-04-21 22:23:11.402122",
                        "event": "reached_pg"
                    },
                    {
                        "time": "2017-04-21 22:23:11.402146",
                        "event": "started"
                    },
                    {
                        "time": "2017-04-21 22:23:11.402177",
                        "event": "waiting for subops from 14,37"
                    },
                    {
                        "time": "2017-04-21 22:23:11.402368",
                        "event": "commit_queued_for_journal_write"
                    },
                    {
                        "time": "2017-04-21 22:23:11.402379",
                        "event": "write_thread_in_journal_buffer"
                    },
                    {
                        "time": "2017-04-21 22:23:11.402585",
                        "event": "journaled_completion_queued"
                    },
                    {
                        "time": "2017-04-21 22:23:11.402598",
                        "event": "op_commit"
                    }
```

From the previous example IO, we can see all the stages that are logged for each operation; it is clear that this operation is running without any performance problems. However, in the event of slow performance, you may see a large delay between two steps, and directing your investigation into this area may lead you to the route cause.

Extremely slow performance or no IO

If your cluster is performing really slowly, to the point that it is barely servicing IO requests, then there is probably an underlying fault or configuration issue. These slow requests will likely be highlighted on the Ceph status display with a counter for how long the request has been blocked. There are a number of things to check in this case.

Flapping OSDs

Check `ceph.log` on the monitors, and see whether it looks like any OSDs are flapping up and down. When an OSD joins a cluster, its PGs begin peering. During this peering process, IO is temporarily halted, so in the event of a number of OSD's flapping, the client IO can be severely impacted. If there is evidence of flapping OSDs, the next step is to go through the logs for the OSDs that are flapping, and see whether there are any clues as to what is causing them to flap. Flapping OSDs can be tough to track down as there can be several different causes, and the problem can be widespread.

Jumbo frames

Check that a network change hasn't caused problems with jumbo frames if in use. If jumbo frames are not working correctly, smaller packets will most likely be successfully getting through to other OSDs and MONs, but larger packets will be dropped. This will result in OSDs that appear to be half functioning, and it can be very difficult to find an obvious cause. If something odd seems to be happening, always check that jumbo frames are being allowed across your network using ping.

Failing disks

As Ceph stripes data across all disks in the cluster, a single disk, which is in the process of failing but has not yet completely failed, may start to cause slow or blocked IO across the cluster. Often, this will be caused by a disk that is suffering from a large number of read errors, but it is not severe enough for the disk to completely fail. Normally, a disk will only reallocate sectors when a bad sector is written to. Monitoring the SMART stats from the disks will normally pick up conditions such as these and allow you to take action.

Slow OSDs

Sometimes an OSD may start performing very poorly for no apparent reason. If there is nothing obvious being revealed by your monitoring tools, consult `ceph.log` and the Ceph health detail output. You can also run Ceph `osd perf`, which will list all the commit and apply latencies of all your OSDs and may also help you identify a problematic OSD.
If there is a common pattern of OSDs referenced in the slow requests, then there is a good chance that the mentioned OSD is the cause of the problems. It is probably worth restarting the OSD in case that resolves the issue; if the OSD is still problematic, it would be advisable to mark it out and then replace the OSD.

Investigating PGs in a down state

A PG in a down state will not service any client operations, and any object contained within the PG will be unavailable. This will cause slow requests to build up across the cluster as clients try to access these objects. The most common reason for a PG to be in a down state is when a number of OSDs are offline, which means that there are no valid copies of the PGs on any active OSDs. However, to find out why a PG is down, you can run the following command:

```
ceph pg x.y query
```

This will produce a large amount of output; the section we are interested in shows the peering status. The example here was taken from a PG whose pool was set to `min_size` 1 and had data written to it when only OSD 0 was up and running. OSD 0 was then stopped and OSDs 1 and 2 were started.

```
    "probing_osds": [
        "1",
        "2"
    ],
    "blocked": "peering is blocked due to down osds",
    "down_osds_we_would_probe": [
        0
    ],
    "peering_blocked_by": [
        {
            "osd": 0,
            "current_lost_at": 0,
            "comment": "starting or marking this osd lost may let us proceed"
        }
    ]
},
```

We can see that the peering process is being blocked, as Ceph knows that the PG has newer data written to OSD 0. It has probed OSDs 1 and 2 for the data, which means that it didn't find anything it needed. It wants to try and pol OSD 0, but it can't because the OSD is down, hence the message **starting or marking this osd lost may let us proceed** appeared.

Large monitor databases

Ceph monitors use `leveldb` to store all of the required monitor data for your cluster. This includes things such as the monitor map, OSD map, and PG map, which OSDs and clients pull from the monitors to be able to locate objects in the RADOS cluster. One particular feature that one should be aware of is that during a period where the health of the cluster doesn't equal `HEALTH_OK`, the monitors do not discard any of the older cluster maps from its database. If the cluster is in a degraded state for an extended period of time and/or the cluster has a large number of OSDs, the monitor database can grow very large.

In normal operating conditions, the monitors are very lightweight on resource consumption; because of this, it's quite common for smaller disk sizes to be used for the monitors. In the scenario where a degraded condition continues for an extended period, it's possible for the disk holding the monitor database to fill up, which, if it occurs across all your monitor nodes, will take down the entire cluster.

To guard against this behavior, it maybe worth deploying your monitor nodes using LVM so that, in the event the disks need to be expanded, this can be done a lot more easily. When you get into this situation, adding disk space is the only solution, until you can get the rest of your cluster into a `HEALTH_OK` state.

If your cluster is in a `HEALTH_OK` state, but the monitor database is still large, you can compact it by running the following command:

```
sudo ceph tell mon.{id} compact
```

However, this will only work if your cluster is in a `HEALTH_OK` state; the cluster will not discard old cluster maps, which can be compacted, until it's in a `HEALTH_OK` state.

Summary

In this chapter, you learned how to deal with problems that Ceph is not able to solve by itself. You now understand the necessary steps to troubleshoot a variety of issues that, if left unhandled, could escalate into bigger problems. Furthermore, you also have a good idea of the key areas to look at when your Ceph cluster is not performing as expected. You should feel confident that you are now in a much better place to handle Ceph-related issues whenever they appear.

11
Disaster Recovery

In the previous chapter, you learned how to troubleshoot common Ceph problems, which, although may be affecting the operation of the cluster, weren't likely to cause a total outage or data loss. This chapter will cover more serious scenarios where the Ceph cluster is down or unresponsive. It will also cover various techniques to recover from data loss. It is to be understood that these techniques are more than capable of causing severe data loss themselves and should only be attempted as a last resort. If you have a support contract with your Ceph vendor or have a relationship with Red Hat, it is highly advisable to consult them first before carrying out any of the recovery techniques listed in this chapter.

In this chapter, you will learn the following:

- How to avoid data loss
- How to use RBD mirroring to provide highly available block storage
- How to investigate asserts
- How to rebuild monitor dbs from OSDs
- How to extract PGs from a dead OSD
- How to recover from lost objects or inactive PGs
- How to rebuild a RBD from dead OSDs

What is a disaster?

To be able to recover from a disaster, you first have to understand and be able to recognize one. For the purpose of this chapter, we will work with the assumption that anything that leads to a sustained period of downtime is classed as a disaster. This will not cover scenarios where a failure happens that Ceph is actively working to recover from, or where it is believed that the cause is likely to be short lived. The other type of disaster is one that leads to a permanent loss of data unless recovery of the Ceph cluster is possible. Data loss is probably the most serious issue as the data may be irreplaceable or can cause serious harm to the future of the business.

Avoiding data loss

Before starting to cover some recovery techniques, it is important to cover some points discussed in Chapter 1, *Planning for Ceph*. Disaster recovery should be seen as a last resort; the recovery guides in this chapter should not be relied upon as a replacement for following best practices.

Firstly, make sure you have working and tested backups of your data; in the event of an outage you will feel a million times more relaxed if you know that in the worst cases, you can fall back to backups. While an outage may cause discomfort for your users or customers, informing them that their data, which they had entrusted you with, is now gone and is far worse. Also, just because you have a backup system in place, do not blindly put your trust in it. Regular test restores will mean that you will be able to rely on them when needed.

Make sure you follow some design principles also mentioned in Chapter 1, *Planning for Ceph*. Don't use configuration options, such as nobarrier, and strongly consider the replication level you use with in Ceph to protect your data. The chances of data loss are strongly linked to the redundancy level configured in Ceph, so careful planning is advised here.

What can cause an outage or data loss?

The majority of outages and cases of data loss will be directly caused by the loss of a number of OSDs that exceed the replication level in a short period of time. If these OSDs do not come back online, be it due to a software or hardware failure and Ceph was not able to recover objects in-between OSD failures, then these objects are now lost.

If an OSD has failed due to a failed disk, then it is unlikely that recovery will be possible unless costly disk recovery services are utilized, and there is no guarantee that any recovered data will be in a consistent state. This chapter will not cover recovering from physical disk failures and will simply suggest that the default replication level of 3 should be used to protect you against multiple disk failures.

If an OSD has failed due to a software bug, the outcome is possibly a lot more positive, but the process is complex and time-consuming. Usually an OSD, which, although the physical disk is in a good condition is unable to start, is normally linked to either a software bug or some form of corruption. A software bug may be triggered by an uncaught exception that leaves the OSD in a state that it cannot recover from. Corruption may occur after an unexpected loss of power where the hardware or software was not correctly configured to maintain data consistency. In both cases, the outlook for the OSD itself is probably terminal, and if the cluster has managed to recover from the lost OSDs, it's best just to erase and reintroduce the OSD as an empty disk.

If the number of offline OSDs has meant that all copies of an object are offline, then recovery procedures should be attempted to try and extract the objects from the failed OSDs, and insert them back into the cluster.

RBD mirroring

As mentioned previously, working backups are a key strategy in ensuring that a failure does not result in the loss of data. Starting with the Jewel release, Ceph introduced RBD mirroring, which allows you to asynchronously mirror an RBD from one cluster to another. Note the difference between Cephs native replication, which is synchronous, and RBD mirroring. With synchronous replication, low latency between peers is essential, and asynchronous replication allows the two Ceph clusters to be geographically remote, as latency is no longer a factor.

By having a replicated copy of your RBD images on a separate cluster, you can dramatically reduce both your **Recovery Time Objective (RTO)** and **Recovery Point Objective (RPO)**. The RTO is a measure of how long it takes from initiating recovery to when the data is usable. It is the worst case measurement of time between each data point and describes the expected data loss. A daily backup would have an RPO of 24 hours; for example, potentially, any data written up to 24 hours since the last backup would be lost if you had to restore from a backup.

With RBD mirroring, data is asynchronously replicated to the target RBD, and so, in most cases, the RPO should be under a minute. As the target RBD is also a replica and not a backup that would require to be first restored, the RTO is also likely going to be extremely low. Additionally, as the target RBD is stored on a separate Ceph cluster, it offers additional protection over snapshots, which could also be impacted if the Ceph cluster itself experiences issues. At first glance, this makes RBD mirroring seem like the perfect tool to protect against data loss, and in most cases, it is a very useful tool. RBD mirroring is not a replacement for a proper backup routine though. In the cases where data loss is caused by actions internal to the RBD, such as file system corruption or user error, these changes will be replicated to the target RBD. A separate isolated copy of your data is vital.

With that said, let's take a closer look into how RBD mirroring works.

The journal

One of the key components in RBD mirroring is the journal. The RBD mirroring journal stores all writes to the RBD and acknowledges to the client once they have been written. These writes are then written to the primary RBD image. The journal itself is stored as RADOS objects, prefixed similarly to how RBD images are. Separately, the remote `rbd-mirror` daemon polls the configured RBD mirrors and pulls the newly written journal objects across to the target cluster and replays them into the target RBD.

The rbd-mirror daemon

The `rbd-mirror` daemon is responsible for replaying the contents of the journal to a target RBD in another Ceph cluster. The `rbd-mirror` daemon only needs to run on the target cluster, unless you wish to replicate both ways, in which case, it will need to run on both clusters.

Configuring RBD mirroring

In order to use the RBD mirroring functionality, we will require two Ceph clusters. We could deploy two identical clusters we have been using previously, but the number of VMs involved may exceed the capabilities of what most people's personal machines can run. Therefore, we will modify our vagrant and ansible configuration files to deploy two separate Ceph clusters each with a single monitor and an OSD node.

The required `Vagrantfile` is very similar to the one used in `Chapter 2`, *Deploying Ceph* to deploy your initial test cluster; the hosts part at the top should now look like this:

```
nodes = [
  { :hostname => 'ansible', :ip => '192.168.0.40', :box => 'xenial64' },
    { :hostname => 'site1-mon1', :ip => '192.168.0.41', :box => 'xenial64' },
    { :hostname => 'site2-mon1', :ip => '192.168.0.42', :box => 'xenial64' },
    { :hostname => 'site1-osd1',  :ip => '192.168.0.51', :box => 'xenial64',
:ram => 1024, :osd => 'yes' },
    { :hostname => 'site2-osd1',  :ip => '192.168.0.52', :box => 'xenial64',
:ram => 1024, :osd => 'yes' }
]
```

For the anisble configuration, we will maintain two separate ansible configuration instances so that each cluster can be deployed seperately. We will then maintain separate hosts files per instance, which we will specify when we run the playbook. To do this, we will not copy the `ceph-ansible` files into `/etc/ansible`, but keep them in the home directory.

git clone `https://github.com/ceph/ceph-ansible.git`

```
cp -a ceph-ansible ~/ceph-ansible2
```

Create the same two files called `all` and `Ceph`, in the `group_vars` directory as we did in `Chapter 2`, *Deploying Ceph*. This needs to be done in both copies of `ceph-ansible`:

1. Create a hosts file in each ansible directory, and place the two hosts in each:

```
vagrant@ansible:~/ceph-ansible$ cat hosts
[mons]
site1-mon1

[osds]
site1-osd1

[ceph:children]
mons
osds
```

The above image is for host one and the below image is for the second host

```
vagrant@ansible:~/ceph-ansible2$ cat hosts
[mons]
site2-mon1

[osds]
site2-osd1

[ceph:children]
mons
osds
```

2. Then, run the `site.yml` playbook under each `ceph-ansible` instance to deploy our two Ceph clusters:

   ```
   ansible-playbook -K -i hosts site.yml
   ```

3. Before we can continue with the configuration of the RBD mirroring, we need to adjust the replication level of the default pools to 1, as our clusters only have 1 OSD. Run these commands on both the clusters:

```
vagrant@site1-mon1:~$ sudo ceph osd pool set rbd size 1
set pool 0 size to 1
vagrant@site1-mon1:~$ sudo ceph osd pool set rbd min_size 1
set pool 0 min_size to 1
```

4. Now, install the RBD mirroring daemon on both the clusters:

   ```
   sudo apt-get install rbd-mirror
   ```

```
vagrant@mon1:~$ sudo apt-get install rbd-mirror
Reading package lists... Done
Building dependency tree
Reading state information... Done
The following NEW packages will be installed:
  rbd-mirror
0 upgraded, 1 newly installed, 0 to remove and 121 not upgraded.
Need to get 1,726 kB of archives.
After this operation, 7,240 kB of additional disk space will be used.
Get:1 http://download.ceph.com/debian-kraken xenial/main amd64 rbd-mirror amd64 11.2.0-1xenial [1,726 kB]
Fetched 1,726 kB in 1s (1,289 kB/s)
Selecting previously unselected package rbd-mirror.
(Reading database ... 54945 files and directories currently installed.)
Preparing to unpack .../rbd-mirror_11.2.0-1xenial_amd64.deb ...
Unpacking rbd-mirror (11.2.0-1xenial) ...
Processing triggers for ureadahead (0.100.0-19) ...
Processing triggers for man-db (2.7.5-1) ...
Setting up rbd-mirror (11.2.0-1xenial) ...
ceph-rbd-mirror.target is a disabled or a static unit, not starting it.
Processing triggers for ureadahead (0.100.0-19) ...
```

5. In order for the `rbd-mirror` daemon to be able to communicate with both clusters, we need to copy `ceph.conf` and the `keyring` from both the clusters to each other:

6. Copy `ceph.conf` from `site1-mon1` to `site2-mon1` and call it `remote.conf`:

7. Copy `ceph.client.admin.keyring` from `site1-mon1` to `site2-mon1` and call it `remote.client.admin.keyring`:

8. Repeat these two steps but this time copy the files from `site2-mon1` to `site1-mon1`:

9. Remember to make sure the keyrings are owned by `ceph:ceph`:

```
sudo chown ceph:ceph /etc/ceph/remote.client.admin.keyring
```

10. Now, we need to tell Ceph that the pool called rbd should have the mirroring function enabled:

```
sudo rbd --cluster ceph mirror pool enable rbd image
```

11. Repeat this for the target cluster:

```
sudo rbd --cluster remote mirror pool enable rbd image
```

12. Add the target cluster as a peer of the pool mirroring configuration:

```
sudo rbd --cluster ceph mirror pool peer add rbd
client.admin@remote
```

13. Run the same command locally on the second Ceph cluster as well:

```
sudo rbd --cluster ceph mirror pool peer add rbd
client.admin@remote
```

14. Back on the first cluster, let's create a test RBD to use with our mirroring lab:

```
sudo rbd create mirror_test --size=1G
```

15. Enable the journaling feature on the RBD image:

```
sudo rbd feature enable rbd/mirror_test journaling
```

16. Finally, enable mirroring for the RBD:

```
sudo rbd mirror image enable rbd/mirror_test
```

```
vagrant@site1-mon1:~$ sudo rbd mirror image enable rbd/mirror_test
Mirroring enabled
```

It's important to note that RBD mirroring works via a pull system. The `rbd-mirror` daemon needs to run on the cluster that you wish to mirror the RBDs to; it then connects to the source cluster and pulls the RBDs across. If you were intending to implement a two-way replication where each Ceph cluster replicates with each other, then you would run the `rbd-mirror` daemon on both the clusters. With this in mind, let's enable and start the systemd service for `rbd-mirror` on your target host:

```
sudo systemctl enable ceph-rbd-mirror@admin
sudo systemctl start ceph-rbd-mirror@admin
```

The `rbd-mirror` daemon will now start processing all the RBD images configured for mirroring on your primary cluster.

We can confirm that everything is working as expected by running the following command on the target cluster:

```
sudo rbd --cluster remote mirror pool status rbd -verbose
```

```
vagrant@site1-mon1:~$ sudo rbd --cluster remote mirror pool status rbd --verbose
health: OK
images: 1 total
    1 replaying

mirror_test:
  global_id:   a90b307a-98ec-4835-9ea8-fc2f91b4ae37
  state:       up+replaying
  description: replaying, master_position=[object_number=3, tag_tid=1, entry_tid=2607], mirror_position=
[object_number=3, tag_tid=1, entry_tid=2607], entries_behind_master=0
  last_update: 2017-04-17 14:37:09
```

In the previous screenshot, we can see that our `mirror_test` RBD is in a **up+replaying** state; this means that mirroring is in progress, and we can see via `entries_behind_master` that it is currently up-to-date.

Also note the difference in the output of the RBD `info` commands on either of the clusters. On the source cluster, the primary status is true, which allows you to determine which cluster the RBD is the master state and can be used by clients. This also confirms that although we only created the RBD on the primary cluster, it has been replicated to the secondary one.

The source cluster is shown here:

```
rbd image 'mirror_test':
        size 1024 MB in 256 objects
        order 22 (4096 kB objects)
        block_name_prefix: rbd_data.374b74b0dc51
        format: 2
        features: layering, exclusive-lock, object-map, fast-diff, deep-flatten, journaling
        flags:
        journal: 374b74b0dc51
        mirroring state: enabled
        mirroring global id: a90b307a-98ec-4835-9ea8-fc2f91b4ae37
        mirroring primary: true
```

The target cluster is shown here:

```
rbd image 'mirror_test':
        size 1024 MB in 256 objects
        order 22 (4096 kB objects)
        block_name_prefix: rbd_data.377d2eb141f2
        format: 2
        features: layering, exclusive-lock, object-map, fast-diff, deep-flatten, journaling
        flags:
        journal: 377d2eb141f2
        mirroring state: enabled
        mirroring global id: a90b307a-98ec-4835-9ea8-fc2f91b4ae37
        mirroring primary: false
```

Performing RBD failover

Before we failover the RBD to the secondary cluster, let's map it, create a file system, and place a file on it, so we can confirm that the mirroring is working correctly. As of Linux kernel 4.11, the kernel RBD driver does not support the RBD journaling feature required for RBD mirroring; this means you cannot map the RBD using the kernel RBD client. As such, we will need to use the rbd-nbd utility, which uses the librbd driver in combination with Linux nbd devices to map RBDs via user space. Although there are many things which may cause Ceph to experience slow performance, here are some of the most likely causes.

```
sudo rbd-nbd map mirror_test
```

```
vagrant@site1-mon1:~$ sudo rbd-nbd map mirror_test
/dev/nbd0
```

```
sudo mkfs.ext4 /dev/nbd0
```

```
vagrant@site1-mon1:~$ sudo mkfs.ext4 /dev/nbd0
mke2fs 1.42.13 (17-May-2015)
Discarding device blocks: done
Creating filesystem with 262144 4k blocks and 65536 inodes
Filesystem UUID: d4ff2036-a10b-4003-8a0a-144b0863b55a
Superblock backups stored on blocks:
        32768, 98304, 163840, 229376

Allocating group tables: done
Writing inode tables: done
Creating journal (8192 blocks): done
Writing superblocks and filesystem accounting information: done
```

```
sudo mount /dev/nbd0 /mnt
echo This is a test | sudo tee /mnt/test.txt
sudo umount /mnt
sudo rbd-nbd unmap /dev/nbd0
Now lets demote the RBD on the primary cluster and promote it on the
secondary
sudo rbd --cluster ceph mirror image demote rbd/mirror_test
sudo rbd --cluster remote mirror image promote rbd/mirror_test
```

Now, map and mount the RBD on the secondary cluster, and you should be able to read the test text file that you created on the primary cluster:

```
vagrant@site2-mon1:~$ sudo rbd-nbd map mirror_test
/dev/nbd0
vagrant@site2-mon1:~$ sudo mount /dev/nbd0 /mnt
vagrant@site2-mon1:~$ cat /mnt/test.txt
This is a test
```

We can clearly see that the RBD has successfully been mirrored to the secondary cluster, and the file system content is just as we left it on the primary cluster.

 If you try and map and mount the RBD on the cluster where the RBD is not in the primary state, the operation will just hang, as Ceph will not permit IO to an RBD image in a non-master state.

This concludes the section on RBD mirroring.

RBD recovery

In the event that a number of OSDs have failed, and you are unable to recover them via the `ceph-object-store` tool, your cluster will most likely be in a state where most, if not all, RBD images are inaccessible. However, there is still a chance that you may be able to recover RBD data from the disks in your Ceph cluster. There are tools that can search through the OSD data structure, find the object files relating to RBDs, and then assemble these objects back into a disk image, resembling the original RBD image.

In this section, we will focus on a tool by *Lennart Bader* to recover a test RBD image from our test Ceph cluster. The tool allows the recovery of RBD images from the contents of Ceph OSDs, without any requirement that the OSD is in a running or usable state. It should be noted that if the OSD has been corrupted due to an underlying file system corruption, the contents of the RBD image may still be corrupt. The RBD recovery tool can be found in the following github repository:

```
https://gitlab.lbader.de/kryptur/ceph-recovery
```

Before we start, make sure you have a small test RBD with a valid file system created on your Ceph cluster. Due to the size of the disks in the test environment that we created in `Chapter 2`, *Deploying Ceph*, it is recommended that the RBD is only a gigabyte in size.

We will perform the recovery on one of the monitor nodes, but in practice, this recovery procedure can be done from any node that can access the Ceph OSD disks. To access the disks, we need to make sure that the recovery server has sufficient space to recover the data.

In this example, we will mount the remote OSDs contents via `sshfs`, which allows you to mount remote directories over `ssh`. However in real life, there is nothing to stop you from physically inserting disks into another server or whatever method is required. The tool only requires to see the OSDs data directories:

1. First, we need to clone the Ceph recovery tool from the Git repository.

git clone `https://gitlab.lbader.de/kryptur/ceph-recovery.git`

```
vagrant@mon1:~$ git clone https://gitlab.lbader.de/kryptur/ceph-recovery.git
Cloning into 'ceph-recovery'...
remote: Counting objects: 18, done.
remote: Compressing objects: 100% (18/18), done.
remote: Total 18 (delta 6), reused 0 (delta 0)
Unpacking objects: 100% (18/18), done.
Checking connectivity... done.
```

2. Also, make sure you have `sshfs` installed:

```
sudo apt-get install sshfs
```

```
vagrant@mon1:~$ sudo apt-get install sshfs
Reading package lists... Done
Building dependency tree
Reading state information... Done
The following packages were automatically installed and are no longer required:
  libboost-iostreams1.58.0 libboost-program-options1.58.0 libboost-random1.58.0 libboost-regex1.58.0 libboost-system1.58.0
  libboost-thread1.58.0 libcephfs1 libfcgi0ldbl
Use 'sudo apt autoremove' to remove them.
The following NEW packages will be installed:
  sshfs
0 upgraded, 1 newly installed, 0 to remove and 103 not upgraded.
Need to get 41.7 kB of archives.
After this operation, 138 kB of additional disk space will be used.
Get:1 http://us.archive.ubuntu.com/ubuntu xenial/universe amd64 sshfs amd64 2.5-1ubuntu1 [41.7 kB]
Fetched 41.7 kB in 0s (109 kB/s)
Selecting previously unselected package sshfs.
(Reading database ... 40714 files and directories currently installed.)
Preparing to unpack .../sshfs_2.5-1ubuntu1_amd64.deb ...
Unpacking sshfs (2.5-1ubuntu1) ...
Processing triggers for man-db (2.7.5-1) ...
Setting up sshfs (2.5-1ubuntu1) ...
```

3. Change into the cloned tool directory, and create the empty directories for each of the OSDs:

```
cd ceph-recovery

sudo mkdir osds

sudo mkdir osds/ceph-0

sudo mkdir osds/ceph-1

sudo mkdir osds/ceph-2
```

Now, mount each remote OSD to the directories that we have just created. Note that you need to make sure your OSD directories match your actual test cluster:

```
sudo sshfs vagrant@osd1:/var/lib/ceph/osd/ceph-0 osds/ceph-0

sudo sshfs vagrant@osd2:/var/lib/ceph/osd/ceph-2 osds/ceph-2

sudo sshfs vagrant@osd3:/var/lib/ceph/osd/ceph-1 osds/ceph-1
```

Now, we can use the tool to scan the OSD directories and compile a list of the RBDs that are available. The only parameter needed for this command is the location where the OSDs are mounted. In this case, it is in a directory called `osds`. The results will be listed in the VM directory:

```
sudo ./collect_files.sh osds
```

```
vagrant@mon1:~/ceph-recovery$ sudo ./collect_files.sh osds
Scanning ceph-0
Scanning ceph-1
Scanning ceph-2
Preparing UDATA files
UDATA files ready
Extracting VM IDs
VM IDs extracted
```

If we look inside the VM directory, we can see that the tool has found our test RBD image. Now that we have located the image, the next step is to assemble various objects located on the OSDs. The three parameters for this command are the name of the RBD image found in the previous step, the size of the image, and the destination for the recovered image file. The size of the image is specified in bytes, and it is important that it is at least as big as the original image; it can be bigger, but the RBD will not recover if the size is smaller:

```
sudo ./assemble.sh vms/test.id 1073741824 .
```

```
vagrant@mon1:~/ceph-recovery$ sudo ./assemble.sh vms/test.id 1073741824 .
1e502238e1f29
test
file_lists/1e502238e1f29.files
---------------------------
CEPH RECOVERY
Assemble test with ID 1e502238e1f29
---------------------------
Searching file list
file_lists/1e502238e1f29.files found
---------------------------
Output Image will be ./test.raw
---------------------------
There are 15 blocks found
The output file will be created as a file of size 1073741824 Bytes
The blocksize is 512
---------------------------
Creating Image file...
Starting reassembly...
100% [##################################################################################_]
Image written to ./test.raw
```

The RBD will now be recovered from the mounted OSD contents to the specified image file. Depending on the size of the image, it may take a while, and a progress bar will show you its progress.

Once completed, we can run a file system called `fsck` on the image to make sure that it has been recovered correctly. In this case, the RBD was formatted with `ext4`, so we can use the `e2fsck` tool to check the image:

```
sudo e2fsck test.raw
```

```
vagrant@mon1:~/ceph-recovery$ sudo e2fsck test.raw
e2fsck 1.42.13 (17-May-2015)
test.raw: clean, 11/65536 files, 12635/262144 blocks
```

Excellent, the image file is clean, which means that there is now a very high chance that all our data has been recovered successfully.

Now, we can finally mount the image as a loop-back device to access our data. If the command returns no output, then we have successfully mounted it:

```
sudo mount -o loop test.raw /mnt
```

You can see that the image is successfully mounted as a loop device:

```
vagrant@mon1:~/ceph-recovery$ df -h
Filesystem                  Size  Used Avail Use% Mounted on
udev                        225M     0  225M   0% /dev
tmpfs                        49M  5.7M   44M  12% /run
/dev/mapper/vagrant--vg-root 38G  2.6G   34G   8% /
tmpfs                       245M     0  245M   0% /dev/shm
tmpfs                       5.0M     0  5.0M   0% /run/lock
tmpfs                       245M     0  245M   0% /sys/fs/cgroup
/dev/sda1                   472M   57M  391M  13% /boot
vagrant                     238G   95G  144G  40% /vagrant
tmpfs                        49M     0   49M   0% /run/user/1000
/dev/loop0                  976M  1.3M  908M   1% /mnt
```

This concludes the process for recovering RBD images from dead Ceph OSDs.

Lost objects and inactive PGs

This section of the chapter will cover the scenario where a number of OSDs may have gone offline in a short period of time, leaving some objects with no valid replica copies. It's important to note that there is a difference between an object that has no remaining copies and an object that has a remaining copy, but it is known that another copy has had more recent writes. The latter is normally seen when running the cluster with `min_size` set to 1.

To demonstrate how to recover an object that has an out-of-date copy of data, let's perform a series of steps to break the cluster:

1. First, let's set `min_size` to 1; hopefully by the end of this example, you will see why you don't ever want to do this in real life:

   ```
   sudo ceph osd pool set rbd min_size 1
   ```

   ```
   vagrant@mon1:~/ceph-recovery$ sudo ceph osd pool set rbd min_size 1
   set pool 0 min_size to 1
   ```

2. Create a test object that we will make later make Ceph believe is lost:

   ```
   sudo rados -p rbd put lost_object logo.png
   sudo ceph osd set norecover
   sudo ceph osd set nobackfill
   ```

   These two flags make sure that when the OSDS come back online after making the write to a single OSD, the changes are not recovered. Since we are only testing with a single option, we need these flags to simulate the condition in real life, where it's likely that not all objects can be recovered in sufficient time before the OSD, when the only copy goes offline for whatever reason.

3. Shut down two of the OSD nodes, so only one OSD is remaining. Since we have set `min_size` to 1, we will still be able to write data to the cluster. You can see that the Ceph status shows that the two OSDS are now down:

   ```
   cluster d9f58afd-3e62-4493-ba80-0356290b3d9f
    health HEALTH_WARN
           64 pgs degraded
           26 pgs stuck unclean
           64 pgs undersized
           recovery 46/69 objects degraded (66.667%)
           too few PGs per OSD (21 < min 30)
           2/3 in osds are down
           nobackfill,norecover flag(s) set
           all OSDs are running kraken or later but the 'require_kraken_osds' osdmap flag is not set
    monmap e2: 3 mons at {mon1=192.168.0.41:6789/0,mon2=192.168.0.42:6789/0,mon3=192.168.0.43:6789/0}
           election epoch 258, quorum 0,1,2 mon1,mon2,mon3
       mgr active: mon1 standbys: mon2, mon3
    osdmap e398: 3 osds: 1 up, 3 in; 64 remapped pgs
           flags nobackfill,norecover,sortbitwise,require_jewel_osds
     pgmap v5286: 64 pgs, 1 pools, 37579 kB data, 23 objects
           226 MB used, 26668 MB / 26894 MB avail
           46/69 objects degraded (66.667%)
                 64 active+undersized+degraded
   ```

4. Now, write to the object again, the write will go to the remaining OSD:

   ```
   sudo rados -p rbd put lost_object logo.png
   ```

5. Now, shut down the remaining OSDS; once it has gone offline, power back the remaining 2 OSDS:

```
cluster d9f58afd-3e62-4493-ba80-0356290b3d9f
 health HEALTH_WARN
        64 pgs degraded
        1 pgs recovering
        64 pgs stuck unclean
        64 pgs undersized
        recovery 25/69 objects degraded (36.232%)
        recovery 1/23 unfound (4.348%)
        1/3 in osds are down
        all OSDs are running kraken or later but the 'require_kraken_osds' osdmap flag is not set
 monmap e2: 3 mons at {mon1=192.168.0.41:6789/0,mon2=192.168.0.42:6789/0,mon3=192.168.0.43:6789/0}
        election epoch 258, quorum 0,1,2 mon1,mon2,mon3
    mgr active: mon1 standbys: mon2, mon3
 osdmap e409: 3 osds: 2 up, 3 in; 64 remapped pgs
        flags sortbitwise,require_jewel_osds
  pgmap v5319: 64 pgs, 1 pools, 37579 kB data, 23 objects
        220 MB used, 26674 MB / 26894 MB avail
        25/69 objects degraded (36.232%)
        1/23 unfound (4.348%)
             63 active+undersized+degraded
              1 active+recovering+undersized+degraded
```

You can see that Ceph knows that it already has an unfound object even before the recovery process has started. This is because during the peering phase, the PG containing the modified object knows that the only valid copy is on osd.0 ,which is now offline.

6. Remove the nobackfill and norecover flags, and let the cluster try and and perform recovery. You will see that even after the recovery has progressed, there will be 1 PG in a degraded state, and the unfound object warning will still be present. This is a good thing, as Ceph is protecting your data from corruption. Imagine what would happen if a 4 MB chunk of an RBD containing a database suddenly went back in time!

If you try and read or write to our test object, you will notice the request will just hang; this is Ceph again protecting your data. There are three ways to fix this problem. The first solution and the most ideal one is to get a valid copy of this object back online; this could either be done by bringing osd.0 online, or by using the objectstore tool to export and import this object into a healthy OSD. But for the purpose of this section, let's assume that neither of those options is possible. Before we cover the remaining two options, let's investigate further to try and uncover what is going on under-the-hood.

Run the Ceph health detail to find out which PG is having the problem:

```
vagrant@mon1:~$ sudo ceph health detail
HEALTH_WARN 1 pgs degraded; 1 pgs stuck unclean; recovery 2/46 objects degraded (4.348%); recovery 1/
 are running kraken or later but the 'require_kraken_osds' osdmap flag is not set
pg 0.31 is stuck unclean for 1370.786568, current state active+degraded, last acting [2,1]
pg 0.31 is active+degraded, acting [2,1], 1 unfound
recovery 2/46 objects degraded (4.348%)
recovery 1/23 unfound (4.348%)
```

In this case, it's pg `0.31`, which is in a degraded state, because it has an unfound object. Let's query the pg:

```
ceph pg 0.31 query
```

```
"recovery_state": [
    {
        "name": "Started\/Primary\/Active",
        "enter_time": "2017-03-28 21:17:56.412097",
        "might_have_unfound": [
            {
                "osd": "0",
                "status": "osd is down"
            },
            {
                "osd": "1",
                "status": "already probed"
            }
```

Look for the recovery section; we can see that Ceph has tried to probe `"osd": "0"` for the object, but it is down. It has tried to probe `"osd": "1"` for the object, but for whatever reason it was of no use, we know the reason is that it is an out-of-date copy.

Now, let's look into some more detail on the missing object:

```
sudo ceph pg 0.31 list_missing
```

```
vagrant@mon1:~$ sudo ceph pg 0.31 list_missing
{
    "offset": {
        "oid": "",
        "key": "",
        "snapid": 0,
        "hash": 0,
        "max": 0,
        "pool": -9223372036854775808,
        "namespace": ""
    },
    "num_missing": 1,
    "num_unfound": 1,
    "objects": [
        {
            "oid": {
                "oid": "lost_object",
                "key": "",
                "snapid": -2,
                "hash": 1434772465,
                "max": 0,
                "pool": 0,
                "namespace": ""
            },
            "need": "398'6",
            "have": "383'5",
            "locations": []
        }
    ],
    "more": false
```

The need and have lines reveal the reason. We have `epoch 383'5`, but the valid copy of the object exists in `398'6`; this is why `min_size=1` is bad. You might be in a situation where you only have a single valid copy of an object. If this was caused by a disk failure, you would have bigger problems.

To recover from this, we have two options: we can either choose to use the older copy of the object or simply delete it. It should be noted that if this object is new and an older copy does not exist on the remaining OSDS, then it will also delete the object.

To delete the object, run this:

```
ceph pg 0.31 mark_unfound_lost delete
```

To revert it, run this:

```
ceph pg 0.31 mark_unfound_lost revert
```

This concludes recovering from unfound objects.

Recovering from a complete monitor failure

In the a unlikely event that you lose all of your monitors, all is not lost. You can rebuild the monitor database from the contents of the OSDs by the use of the `ceph-objectstore` tool.

To set the scenario, we will assume that an event has occurred and has corrupted all three monitors, effectively leaving the Ceph cluster inaccessible. To recover the cluster, we will shut down two of the monitors and leave a single failed monitor running. We will then rebuild the monitor database, overwrite the corrupted copy, and then restart the monitor to bring the Ceph cluster back online.

The `objectstore` tool needs to be able to access every OSD in the cluster to rebuild the monitor database; in this example, we will use a script, which will connect via `ssh` to access the OSD data. As the OSD data is not accessible by every user, we will use the root user to log in to the OSD hosts. By default, most Linux distributions will not allow remote, password-based root logins, so ensure you have copied your public `ssh` key to the root users on some remote OSD nodes.

The following script will connect to each of the OSD nodes specified in the hosts variable, and it will extract the data required to build the monitor database:

```bash
#!/bin/bash
hosts="osd1 osd2 osd3"
ms=/tmp/mon-store/
mkdir $ms
# collect the cluster map from OSDs
for host in $hosts; do
  echo $host
  rsync -avz $ms root@$host:$ms
  rm -rf $ms
  ssh root@$host <<EOF
    for osd in /var/lib/ceph/osd/ceph-*; do
      ceph-objectstore-tool --data-path \$osd --op update-mon-db --mon-store-path $ms
    done
EOF
  rsync -avz root@$host:$ms $ms
done
```

This will generate the following contents in the `/tmp/mon-store` directory:

```
vagrant@mon1:~$ ls /tmp/mon-store/
kv_backend  store.db
```

We also need to assign new permissions via the `keyring`:

```
sudo ceph-authtool /etc/ceph/ceph.client.admin.keyring --create-keyring --gen-key -n client.admin --cap mon 'allow *' --cap osd 'allow *' --cap mds 'allow *'
```

```
vagrant@mon1:~$ sudo ceph-authtool /etc/ceph/ceph.client.admin.keyring --create-keyring --gen-key -n client.admin --cap mon 'allow *' --cap osd 'allow *' --cap mds 'allow *'
creating /etc/ceph/ceph.client.admin.keyring
```

```
sudo ceph-authtool /etc/ceph/ceph.client.admin.keyring --gen-key -n mon. --cap mon 'allow *'
```

```
sudo cat /etc/ceph/ceph.client.admin.keyring
```

```
vagrant@mon1:~$ sudo cat /etc/ceph/ceph.client.admin.keyring
[mon.]
        key = AQBODeBYfJFeIRAALrl1DmvSO16983LxfCsDpA==
        caps mon = "allow *"
[client.admin]
        key = AQAzDeBYbuP+IRAA4mi1ZnbZW41v4F8taiRPHg==
        caps mds = "allow *"
        caps mon = "allow *"
        caps osd = "allow *"
```

Now that the monitor database is rebuilt, we can copy it to the monitor directory, but before we do so, let's take a backup of the existing database:

```
sudo mv /var/lib/ceph/mon/ceph-mon1/store.db /var/lib/ceph/mon/ceph-mon1/store.bak
```

Now, copy the rebuilt version:

```
sudo mv /tmp/mon-store/store.db /var/lib/ceph/mon/ceph-mon1/store.db
sudo chown -R ceph:ceph /var/lib/ceph/mon/ceph-mon1
```

If you try and start the monitor now, it will get stuck in a probing state, as it tries to probe for other monitors. This is Ceph trying to avoid a split-brain scenario; however in this case, we want to force it to form a quorum and go fully online. To do this, we need to edit monmap, remove the other monitors, and then inject it back into the monitors database:

```
sudo ceph-mon -i mon1 --extract-monmap /tmp/monmap
```

Check the contents of the monmap:

```
sudo monmaptool /tmp/monmap -print
```

```
vagrant@mon1:~$ sudo monmaptool /tmp/monmap --print
monmaptool: monmap file /tmp/monmap
epoch 0
fsid d9f58afd-3e62-4493-ba80-0356290b3d9f
last_changed 2017-03-29 21:14:32.762117
created 2017-03-29 21:14:32.762117
0: 192.168.0.41:6789/0 mon.noname-a
1: 192.168.0.42:6789/0 mon.noname-b
2: 192.168.0.43:6789/0 mon.noname-c
```

You will see that there are three mons present, so let's remove two of them:

```
sudo monmaptool /tmp/monmap --rm noname-b
```

```
sudo monmaptool /tmp/monmap --rm noname-c
```

Now, check again to make sure they are completely gone:

```
sudo monmaptool /tmp/monmap -print
```

```
vagrant@mon1:~$ sudo monmaptool /tmp/monmap --print
monmaptool: monmap file /tmp/monmap
epoch 0
fsid d9f58afd-3e62-4493-ba80-0356290b3d9f
last_changed 2017-03-29 21:14:32.762117
created 2017-03-29 21:14:32.762117
0: 192.168.0.41:6789/0 mon.noname-a
```

```
sudo ceph-mon -i mon1 --inject-monmap /tmp/monmap
```

Restart all your OSDs, so they rejoin the cluster; then you will be able to successfully query the cluster status and see that your data is still there:

```
vagrant@mon1:~$ sudo ceph -s
    cluster d9f58afd-3e62-4493-ba80-0356290b3d9f
     health HEALTH_WARN
            all OSDs are running kraken or later but the 'require_kraken_osds' osdmap flag is not set
     monmap e2: 1 mons at {mon1=192.168.0.41:6789/0}
            election epoch 3, quorum 0 mon1
        mgr no daemons active
     osdmap e460: 3 osds: 3 up, 3 in
            flags sortbitwise,require_jewel_osds
      pgmap v90: 64 pgs, 1 pools, 37579 kB data, 23 objects
            174 MB used, 26720 MB / 26894 MB avail
                 64 active+clean
recovery io 199 kB/s, 0 objects/s
vagrant@mon1:~$ sudo rbd ls
test
```

This concludes the section of this chapter on how to recover from a complete monitor failure.

Using the Cephs object store tool

Hopefully, if you have followed best practice, your cluster is running with three replicas and is not configured with any dangerous configuration options. Ceph, in most cases, should be able to recover from any failure.

However, in the scenario where a number of OSDs go offline, a number of PGs and/or objects may become unavailable. If you are unable to reintroduce these OSDs back into the cluster to allow Ceph to recover them gracefully, then the data in those PGs is effectively lost. However, there is a possibility that the OSD is still readable to use the objectstore tool to recover the PGs contents. The process involves exporting the PGs from the failed OSDs and then importing the PGs back into the cluster. The objectstore tool does require that the OSDs internal metadata is still in a consistent state, so full recovery is not guaranteed.

In order to demonstrate the use of the objectstore tool, we will shut down two of our three test cluster OSDs, and then recover the missing PGs back into the cluster. In real life, its unlikely you would be facing a situation where every single PG from the failed OSDs is missing, but for demonstration purposes, the required steps are the same:

1. First, let's set the pool size to 2, so we can make sure that we lose all the copies of some PGs when we stop the OSD service:

```
vagrant@mon1:~$ sudo ceph osd pool set rbd size 2
set pool 0 size to 2
```

2. Now, shut down two of the OSD services, and you will see from the Ceph status screen that the number of PGs will go offline:

```
vagrant@mon1:~$ sudo ceph -s
    cluster d9f58afd-3e62-4493-ba80-0356290b3d9f
     health HEALTH_ERR
            27 pgs are stuck inactive for more than 300 seconds
            64 pgs degraded
            23 pgs stale
            27 pgs stuck inactive
            27 pgs stuck unclean
            64 pgs undersized
            recovery 18/36 objects degraded (50.000%)
            too few PGs per OSD (21 < min 30)
            2/3 in osds are down
     monmap e2: 3 mons at {mon1=192.168.0.41:6789/0,mon2=192.168.0.42:6789/0,mon3=192.168.0.43:6789/0}
            election epoch 10, quorum 0,1,2 mon1,mon2,mon3
        mgr active: mon2 standbys: mon3, mon1
     osdmap e22: 3 osds: 1 up, 3 in; 41 remapped pgs
            flags sortbitwise,require_jewel_osds,require_kraken_osds
      pgmap v105: 64 pgs, 1 pools, 37572 kB data, 18 objects
            233 MB used, 26661 MB / 26894 MB avail
            18/36 objects degraded (50.000%)
                   41 undersized+degraded+peered
                   23 stale+undersized+degraded+peered
```

3. Running a Ceph health detail will also show which PGs are in a degraded state:

```
pg 0.21 is stale+undersized+degraded+peered, acting [2]
pg 0.22 is stale+undersized+degraded+peered, acting [2]
pg 0.23 is stale+undersized+degraded+peered, acting [2]
pg 0.24 is undersized+degraded+peered, acting [0]
pg 0.25 is undersized+degraded+peered, acting [0]
pg 0.26 is undersized+degraded+peered, acting [0]
pg 0.27 is undersized+degraded+peered, acting [0]
pg 0.28 is undersized+degraded+peered, acting [0]
pg 0.29 is undersized+degraded+peered, acting [0]
pg 0.2a is stale+undersized+degraded+peered, acting [2]
pg 0.2b is stale+undersized+degraded+peered, acting [2]
pg 0.2c is undersized+degraded+peered, acting [0]
pg 0.2d is stale+undersized+degraded+peered, acting [2]
```

The stale PGs are the ones that no longer have a surviving copy, and it can be seen that the acting OSD is the one that was shut down.

If we use `grep` to filter out just the stale PGs, we can use the resulting list to work out what PGs we need to recover. If the OSDs have actually been removed from the cluster, then the PGs will be listed as incomplete rather than stale.

4. Check the OSD to make sure the PG exists in it:

```
vagrant@osd3:~$ sudo ls -l /var/lib/ceph/osd/ceph-2/current/0.2d_head
total 0
-rw-r--r-- 1 ceph ceph 0 Apr  2 20:13 __head_0000002D__0
```

5. We will now use the `objectstore` tool to export the pg to a file. As the amount of data in our test cluster is small, we can just export the data to the OS disk. In real life, you probably want to consider connecting additional storage to the server. USB disks are ideal for this, as they can easily be moved between servers as part of the recovery process:

```
sudo ceph-objectstore-tool --op export --pgid 0.2a --data-path
/var/lib/ceph/osd/ceph-2 --file 0.2a_export
```

```
vagrant@osd3:~$ sudo ceph-objectstore-tool --op export --pgid 0.2a --data-path /var/lib/ceph/osd/ceph-2 --file 0.2a_export
Exporting 0.2a
Read #0:54d415a2:::rbd_data.fa68238e1f29.0000000000000060:head#
Export successful
```

If you experience an assert while running the tool, you can try running it with the `--skip-journal-replay` flag, which will skip replaying the journal into the OSD. If there was any outstanding data in the journal, it will be lost. But this may allow you to recover the bulk of the missing PGs that would have otherwise been impossible. And repeat this until you have exported all the missing PGs.

6. Now, we can import the missing PGs back into an operating OSD; while we could import the PGs into an existing OSD, it is much safer to perform the import on a new OSD, so we don't risk further data loss. For this demonstration, we will create a directory-based OSD on the disk used by the failed OSD. It's highly recommended in a real disaster scenario that the data would be inserted into an OSD running on a separate disk, rather than using an existing OSD. This is done so that there is no further risk to any data in the Ceph cluster.

Also, it doesn't matter that the PGs that are being imported are all inserted into the same temporary OSD. As soon as Ceph discovers the objects, it will recover them to the correct location in the cluster.

7. Create a new empty folder for the OSD:

```
sudo mkdir /var/lib/ceph/osd/ceph-2/tmposd/
```

8. Use `ceph-disk` to prepare the directory for Ceph:

```
sudo ceph-disk prepare  /var/lib/ceph/osd/ceph-2/tmposd/
```

9. Change the ownership of the folder to the ceph user and the group:

```
sudo chown -R ceph:ceph /var/lib/ceph/osd/ceph-2/tmposd/
```

10. Activate the OSD to bring it online:

```
sudo ceph-disk activate  /var/lib/ceph/osd/ceph-2/tmposd/
```

11. Set the weight of the OSD to stop any objects from being backfilled into it:

```
sudo ceph osd crush reweight osd.3 0
```

12. Now, we can proceed with the PG import, specifying the temporary OSD location and the PG files that we exported earlier:

```
sudo ceph-objectstore-tool --op import --data-path
/var/lib/ceph/osd/ceph-3 --file 0.2a_export
```

```
vagrant@osd3:~$ sudo ceph-objectstore-tool --op import --data-path /var/lib/ceph/osd/ceph-3 --file 0.2a_export
Importing pgid 0.2a
Write #0:54d415a2:::rbd_data.fa68238e1f29.0000000000000060:head#
Import successful
```

13. Repeat this for every PG that you exported previously. Once complete, reset file onwership and restart the new temp OSD:

```
sudo chown -R ceph:ceph /var/lib/ceph/osd/ceph-2/tmposd/
sudo systemctl start ceph-osd@3
```

14. After checking the Ceph status output, you will see that your PGs are now active, but in a degraded state. In the case of our test cluster, there are not sufficient OSDs to allow the objects to recover to the correct amount of copies. If there were more OSDs in the cluster, the objects would then be backfilled around the cluster and would recover to full health with the correct number of copies.

```
vagrant@mon1:~$ sudo ceph -s
    cluster d9f58afd-3e62-4493-ba80-0356290b3d9f
     health HEALTH_WARN
            clock skew detected on mon.mon2
            41 pgs degraded
            64 pgs stuck unclean
            41 pgs undersized
            recovery 13/36 objects degraded (36.111%)
            recovery 5/36 objects misplaced (13.889%)
            Monitor clock skew detected
     monmap e2: 3 mons at {mon1=192.168.0.41:6789/0,mon2=192.168.0.42:6789/0,mon3=192.168.0.43:6789/0}
            election epoch 10, quorum 0,1,2 mon1,mon2,mon3
        mgr active: mon2 standbys: mon3, mon1
     osdmap e48: 4 osds: 2 up, 2 in; 23 remapped pgs
            flags sortbitwise,require_jewel_osds,require_kraken_osds
      pgmap v182: 64 pgs, 1 pools, 37572 kB data, 18 objects
            1184 MB used, 16744 MB / 17929 MB avail
            13/36 objects degraded (36.111%)
            5/36 objects misplaced (13.889%)
                  41 active+undersized+degraded
                  23 active+remapped
```

Investigating asserts

Assertions are used in Ceph to ensure that during the execution of the code any assumptions that have been made about the operating environment remain true. These assertions are scattered throughout the Ceph code and are designed to catch any conditions that may go on to cause further problems if the code is not stopped.

If you trigger an assertion in Ceph, it's likely that some form of data has a value that is unexpected. This may be caused by some form or corruption or unhandled bug.

If an OSD causes an assert and refuses to start anymore, the usual recommended approach would be to destroy the OSD, recreate it, and then let Ceph backfill objects back to it. If you have a reproducible failure scenario, then it is probably also worth filing a bug in the Ceph bug tracker.

As mentioned several times in this chapter, OSDs can fail either due to hardware faults or soft faults in either the stored data or OSD code. Soft faults are much more likely to affect multiple OSDs at once; if your OSDs have become corrupted due to a power outage, then it's highly likely that more than once OSD will be affected. In the case, where multiple OSDs are failing with asserts and they are causing one or more PG's in the cluster to be offline, simply recreating the OSDs is not an option. The OSDs that are offline contain all the three copies of the PG, and so, recreating the OSDs would make any form of recovery impossible and result in permanent data loss.

First, before attempting the recovery techniques in this chapter, such as exporting and importing PGs, investigation into the asserts should be done. Depending on your technical ability and how much downtime you can tolerate before you need to start focusing on other recovery steps, investigating the asserts may not result in any success. By investigating the assert and looking through the Ceph source referenced by the assert, it may be possible to identify the cause of the assert. If this is possible then a fix can be implemented in the Ceph code to avoid the OSD asserting. Don't be afraid to reach out to the community for help on these matters.

In some cases the OSD corruption may be so severe that even the `objectstore` tool may itself assert when trying to read from the OSD. This will limit the recovery steps outlined in this chapter, and trying to fix the reason behind the assert might be the only option. Although by this point, it is likely that the OSD has sustained heavy corruption, and recovery may not be possible.

Example assert

The following assert was taken from the Ceph user's mailing list:

```
2017-03-02 22:41:32.338290 7f8bfd6d7700 -1 osd/ReplicatedPG.cc: In function
'void ReplicatedPG::hit_set_trim(ReplicatedPG::RepGather*, unsigned int)'
thread 7f8bfd6d7700 time 2017-03-02 22:41:32.335020

osd/ReplicatedPG.cc: 10514: FAILED assert(obc)


ceph version 0.94.7 (d56bdf93ced6b80b07397d57e3fa68fe68304432)
 1: (ceph::__ceph_assert_fail(char const*, char const*, int, char
const*)+0x85) [0xbddac5]
 2: (ReplicatedPG::hit_set_trim(ReplicatedPG::RepGather*, unsigned
int)+0x75f) [0x87e48f]
 3: (ReplicatedPG::hit_set_persist()+0xedb) [0x87f4ab]
 4: (ReplicatedPG::do_op(std::tr1::shared_ptr<OpRequest>&)+0xe3a)
[0x8a0d1a]
 5: (ReplicatedPG::do_request(std::tr1::shared_ptr<OpRequest>&,
ThreadPool::TPHandle&)+0x68a) [0x83be4a]
 6: (OSD::dequeue_op(boost::intrusive_ptr<PG>,
std::tr1::shared_ptr<OpRequest>, ThreadPool::TPHandle&)+0x405) [0x69a5c5]
 7: (OSD::ShardedOpWQ::_process(unsigned int,
ceph::heartbeat_handle_d*)+0x333) [0x69ab33]
 8: (ShardedThreadPool::shardedthreadpool_worker(unsigned int)+0x86f)
[0xbcd1cf]
 9: (ShardedThreadPool::WorkThreadSharded::entry()+0x10) [0xbcf300]
 10: (()+0x7dc5) [0x7f8c1c209dc5]
 11: (clone()+0x6d) [0x7f8c1aceaced]
```

The top part of the assert shows the function from where the assert was triggered and also the line number and file where the assert can be found. In this example, the `hit_set_trim` function is apparently the cause of the assert. We can look into the `ReplicatePG.cc` file around line 10514 to try and understand what might have happened. Note the version of the Ceph release (0.94.7), as the line number in GitHub will only match if you are looking at the same version.

From looking at the code, it appears that the returned value from the `get_object_context` function call is directly passed to the `assert` function. If the value is zero, indicating the object containing the hitset to be trimmed could not be found, then the OSD will assert. From this information, there is a chance that investigation could be done to work out why the object is missing and recover it. Or the `assert` command could be commented out to see if it allows the OSD to continue functioning. In this example, allowing the OSD to continue processing will likely not cause an issue, but in other cases, an assert may be the only thing stopping more serious corruption from occurring. If you don't understand 100% why something is causing an assert, and the impact of any potential change you might make, seek help before continuing.

Summary

In this chapter, you have learned how to troubleshoot Ceph when all looks lost. In the event that Ceph is unable to recover PGs itself, you now understand how to manually rebuild PGs from failed OSDs. You can also rebuild the monitor's database in the event that you lose all of your monitor nodes but still have access to your OSDs. In the event of a complete cluster failure that you are unable to recover from, you also have gone through the process of recreating RBDs from the raw data remaining on your OSDs. Finally, you have configured two separate Ceph clusters and configured replication between them using RBD mirroring to provide a failover option, should you encounter a complete Ceph cluster failure.

Index

M

monitor failure
  recovering 208, 209, 210, 211
monitoring, slow performance
  atop 184
  htop 184
  iostat 183

N

network benchmarking 155, 156, 157
network design
  about 22
  OSD node sizes 24
  price, estimating 25
network interface controllers (NICs) 19
NewStore 53
Non-volatile Memory Express (NVMe) 11
notifiers
  used, in librados application 91, 92, 95

O

object storage daemons (OSD)
  about 9
  upgrading, in test cluster 59, 60, 61
online transaction processing (OLTP) databases
  139
Open Shortest Path First (OSPF) 24
OpenStack Cinder 13
operating system (OS) 32
orchestration 38
OSD node sizes
  failure domains 24
out-of-memory (OOM) 17
outage
  causes 192, 193

P

P-states 162
partial overwrite 72
Paxos 10
ping tool 155
placement groups (PGs)
  about 10
  investigating, in down state 187, 188

playbook
  about 39
  working 44
portable operating system interface (POSIX) 53
promotion throttling
  about 146, 147
  parameters, monitoring 147, 148
  tiering, with erasure-coded pools 148
proxy mode
  about 138
  read-proxy 138
PuTTY 37
Python Imaging Library (PIL) 83

R

RADOS benchmarking 159, 160
RADOS Block Devices (RBD) 9, 139
RADOS class
  about 102
  benefits 97
  build environment, preparing 100
  caveats 110
  client librados applications 104
  example application 97
  testing 108
  writing, for distributed computing 100
  writing, in Lua 98
RBD benchmarking 160, 161
RBD mirroring
  about 193, 194
  configuring 194, 195, 196, 197, 198, 199
  journal 194
  RBD failover, performing 199
  rbd-mirror daemon 194
RBD recovery
  about 201, 202, 203, 204
  reference link 201
read-forward mode 138
read-proxy mode 138
Recovery Point Objective (RPO) 193
Recovery Time Objective (RTO) 193
Reed-Solomon 67
RocksDB 53, 57
Routing on the Host 24

CPSIA information can be obtained
at www.ICGtesting.com
Printed in the USA
FFOW04n2023301017
41703FF

9 781785 888786